Gig Economy: Opportunities to Work Online with Freelance or Remote Smart Working

Daniel D. Coffman

Published by Creafe Publishing, 2023.

While every precaution has been taken in the preparation of this book, the publisher assumes no responsibility for errors or omissions, or for damages resulting from the use of the information contained herein.

GIG ECONOMY: OPPORTUNITIES TO WORK ONLINE WITH FREELANCE OR REMOTE SMART WORKING

First edition. September 15, 2023.

ISBN: 979-8223974604

Written by Daniel D. Coffman.

Also by Daniel D. Coffman

Freelance Consulting: Provide Services to High Ticket Customers. Build and Grow Your own Gig Empire.

Gig Economy: Opportunities to Work Online with Freelance or Remote Smart Working

Work Online: Become a Solopreneur, Start Working Remotely. The Complete Guide to Grow Your Company on the Internet.

Table of Contents

INTRODUCTION

Pairing the expression Gig Economy lately caught my attention. I had not given much thought about it but it's a significant part of what we do as advisers at the employment service market. Where did this phrase gig arise? Musicians refer to their own compensated demonstrations as gigs and very cool men and women refer to their own temporary tasks as gigs. Put another way, the expression "gigging" means getting paid work or being used.

Now a gig may be a temporary task concerning duration of employment. At the employment business, we frequently refer to those duties as both temporary or contract since it's usually for a specified time period. Gigs may be full-time job hours and sometimes they're part-time hours.

Well, with our strong market sitting in 4.0% unemployment it looks like all is well when it comes to finding employment. Many economists consider these amounts to be misleading. The sensation of wealth isn't being felt by many and this contributes to the requirement to accept an excess job [or 2] by countless Americans simply to make ends meet. We all know by looking at the data which folks have a tendency to change jobs many times during their working lives and the gig market can be viewed as a development of the tendency.

In the employment business, we all know that 1 in 5 employees in the work force is flexible or contingent hourly labour. Many professionals are selecting contract employment due to the flexible work hours, work-life equilibrium or a means to remain engaged in the work force whilst maintaining their technical and people skills sharp. While employment amounts rely on W-2 statements these workers may be working part-time or functioning this mission before a better opportunity comes along. There are roughly 6 million individuals [4 percent of labour force] which compose the U.S. based workforce since these amounts have never been monitored in previous decades.

Capturing The gig market is important when working to comprehend the job numbers. Many companies are picking a contingent workforce since they search for ways to stay competitive when controlling labor expenses and expenses. When advertising or seasonal changes impact sales businesses are aware that a contingent workforce lets them stay flexible and rewarding.

"The Gig market isn't new-people have constantly labored gigs ... but now when most men and women refer to this "gig market" they are specifically talking about brand new technology-enabled types of job" I.e Uber, Pinot's Palette, Airbnb, respectively

Firms Should be aware that the increase of the gig market is a worldwide trend and this tendency doesn't show signs of slowing. People are searching for ways to locate balance in their own lives while providing for their own families. Sometimes that needs another job. As we examine these gig employees' businesses we ought to know that these amounts had grown from 4 million to over 9 million in 2021.

Believe tanks, government officials and everybody in between are attempting to find a deal on the gig market. That's the freelancer and builder economy. There are studies which assert that by 2020, in excess of 40% of their U.S. labor force will probably be self-explanatory. I will leave it to the pros to debate their methods and also what proportion of our work force is currently independently employed.

But, I will say that by a single step, IRS 1099 (independent contractors) versions have grown from the 2000s. So also have those that are filing Schedule C (self-employment) in their tax forms.

The Trends and Forces

One Of the most debated studies was just printed by Intuit. And if we will be at 50 percent, 30 percent or not, the simple fact of the matter is that we're going toward a workforce which really will be more flexible. It is on everybody's shoulders to comprehend the changes and trends which are occurring in the hiring picture. I believe a number of the things from this specific research are absolutely on stage.

1. Tech Generations: We Are Living in an electronic world filled with technology. Meaning that everybody is, in reality, competing with all

the younger generations who have had tech in their whole lives. And every generation that develops into maturity is only going to be better at engineering and ready to adapt faster.

2. Baby Boomers Aren't Bowing Out: On the opposite side of this spectrum, we are living in a world in which the senior creation isn't bowing to retirement. Boomers are pursuing new careers and starting their own companies. They are busy and they aren't retiring. To put it differently, they're also competition.

3. The growth of the Voice of Men: In a globalized world, and one which is wired and wired there's a movement for girls throughout the world to undertake leadership roles. According to Booz & Company, over 870 million girls around the planet are going into the workforce or launching new companies. These girls weren't a part of the market that existed as late as the early 2000's.

4. The Glocal Earth: We are living in a wired and connected planet. I really don't think there is any dispute about that. However, since more people enter the discussions, that usually means the world isn't likely to be more dominated, since it had been for so many decades, from Western ideas and culture. There will be a larger emphasis on showing to the world how local cultures and nations around the world do business.

5. Cities Attract Opportunities: As an increasing number of individuals enter the international market they'll find opportunities which are offered to them in urban centres. So inhabitants will continue to move to cities.

6. Social Networking: We see this again and again. Social networking, in its heart, is social media. Meaning that more individuals will be getting their advice and work opportunities utilizing social media (e.g. social websites).

7. People Will Be Accountable for Themselves: I believe among the most important things is that this fact. Gone are the times where employees were shielded by a business (or authorities). Folks are the masters of their own professions and opportunities. Meaning that it drops upon the employees, not companies and not authorities which are cutting social services, to locate their work route, health insurance

and retirement.

Gen Z Is about The Gig Economy

In 2017 we're a year nearer in hot Gen Z to the office. Millennials (Gen Y) have established a safe place and are directing the series, they'll now have to equip themselves to mind the newcomer.

With this change in the creation, HR will have to start its preparation to adopt the new wave of staffing in the authentic digital natives (Gen Z). Gen Z is in continuous touch with all the electronic world and it's fairly impossible to isolate them. This new alliance with new talent does not come that simple. Recruiters have to check at the on-boarding of the Production as a potential organizational disturbance and reevaluate business operations and management to best engage the post-millennials.

The modern job market sees recruiting teams and supervisors hiring more workers that are booming. In 2015, a research from Ardent's research underlined the fact that by 2017 almost 45 percent of the planet's workforce will be identified employees. The characteristics Gen Z conveys manifests the fact they are already being affected by the gig market of independent contractors, contractors, consultants and advisers.

Some Particularities that place Gen Z apart from the rest and sends their taste to the gig market are:

• Individuality:

Individuality And the impulse to standout come naturally with this Production. They hunt jobs that best matches them would not settle down to anything less. An disappointing job means moving to another.

• Multi-tasking:

With Uncertainty always surrounding Gen Z, that they tend to change and with this comes the capacity to overcome the ability to multi-task effectively. The capability to work simultaneously means more hands on experience with numerous jobs and also a wider portfolio to display.

- Top Expectations:

Gen Z is inborn modernizers having a curious nature to understand and research. Job satisfaction is more than just the paycheck they take house, it is about relaxation, work environment and organizational versatility. This kind of outlook might be the reason this Production favors freelancing or work at home, because they may work in their own terms and in their own time advantage.

- Traveling Buffs:

Gen Z is international, they're incessant using their ancestral link. Keenness to research and journey make them more receptive to tasks throughout the world and are always prepared to relocate.

- Tech Savvy:

With Continuous up-gradations and being besieged by electronic devices all of the time, Gen Z is quite much Tech Savvy. They have the net at their hands and learning is now effortless. They could accommodate readily and are extremely agile.

The Time accessible today is insufficient and only around the corner, we've got a lot of determined individuals that hope to make the world a better location. It currently lies upon the shoulders of HR to perform their assignments and examine the potential and the chances Gen Z could bring to this hyper-competitive job marketplace.

Ever heard of this"Gig" Economy?

In a nutshell, it is a workforce which goes from 1 job"gig" into another, becoming paid under or above the table. ("freelancing" is a variant on this) Though its roots are musical, it's come to define individual contracting at work. In a recent post, Dave Ashton of SnapCar created an argument for replacing certain kinds of classic workers with builders. Make no mistake, he chooses a contentious political situation, more clear perhaps once you realize it is predicated on the French market rather than the USA.

His general point is that the sector is served with independent contractors compared to workers in certain places. It is a Randian office utopia perspective - which when everyone acts in their self-interest all the time, everybody is served. Employees are more efficient since they typically work harder because their earnings directly relates to their own activities, AND they web longer take-home pay. Obviously it is also better for companies because they want fewer workers for whom they cover government-mandated taxes for rewards.

CHAPTER ONE:
WHAT IS GIG ECONOMY?

A Gig market is a free market system where temporary places are typical and associations deal with separate employees for short term engagements. The expression"gig" is a slang word meaning"a project for a predetermined period of time" and is normally utilized in speaking to artists. Examples of gig workers in the workforce may comprise accountants, independent contractors, project-based employees and temporary or part-time jobs.

The tendency toward a gig market has started as a research by Intuit predicted that by 2020, 40 percent of American employees are independent contractors. There are a range of forces behind the development in short term jobs. For starters, in the electronic era, the work force is increasingly mobile and operate can progressively be performed from anywhere, in order that location and job are decoupled. That usually means that freelancers can pick one of temporary jobs and jobs around the planet, while companies can pick the best people for certain jobs from a bigger pool than that available in any particular area.

Digitization has also donated directly to a reduction in jobs as applications simplifies some varieties of work to maximize time efficiency. Other impacts include monetary pressures on companies causing a flexible workforce and also the entry of their Milennial production into the labour market. The present reality is that folks have a tendency to change jobs many times during their working lives and the gig market can be considered a development of this trend.

In a gig market, companies save funds concerning benefits, office space and instruction. They also have the capability to contract with specialists for certain jobs who may be overly high-priced to keep on employees. From the point of view of the freelancer, a gig market can enhance work-life equilibrium over what's possible in many jobs. The design is powered by separate employees selecting jobs they're interested in, instead of one where individuals are forced to a situation where, not able to achieve employmentthey pick up whatever temporary gigs they could land.

The Gig market is part of a changing cultural and business environment which also contains the sharing market, the present market and the barter economy.

In A gig market, temporary, flexible tasks are commonplace and businesses tend toward hiring independent contractors and contractors rather than full-time workers. A gig market undermines the conventional market of full-time employees who seldom change positions and rather concentrate on a life career.

KEY TAKEAWAYS

- The Gig market relies on flexible, temporary, or freelancer jobs, frequently involving linking with customers or clients through an internet platform.

- The Gig market can benefit employees, companies, and customers by making work more flexible to the requirements of the second and requirement for flexible lifestyles.

- At The exact same time, the gig market can have disadvantages on account of the erosion of conventional financial relationships between employees, companies, and customers.

Recognizing the Gig Economy

In a gig market, large numbers of individuals work part-time or temporary places. The end result of a gig market is more economical, more efficient solutions, for example Uber or even Airbnb, for people willing to utilize them. People of us who don't participate in utilizing technological services like the Internet are inclined to get left behind from the advantages of the gig market. Cities generally have the most highly developed providers and therefore are the most entrenched from the gig market.

There is a broad variety of places that fall in the kind of a gig. By way of instance, adjunct and part-time professors have been contracted workers instead of tenured or tenure-track professors. Colleges and universities may cut prices and match professors for their own academic needs by employing more adjunct and part-time professors.

The Factors of a Gig Economy

America is well on its way to creating a gig market, and estimates reveal up to a third of the working population is currently in certain gig capability. Experts anticipate this functioning number to grow. In today's digital world, it is becoming more and more common for individuals to work remotely or in the home. This eases independent contracting job as most of these jobs do not need the freelancer to come into the office to get the job done. Employers have a broader array of applicants to pick from since they do not need to hire somebody based on their proximity. Furthermore, computers have grown to the stage they can take the place of their tasks people previously stored.

Economic reasons also factor into the growth of a gig market. Most times, companies cannot afford to employ full-time workers to perform all of the work they want done, so that they employ temporary or part-time workers to deal with busier times or particular jobs. On the face of the worker, we often find they should maneuver around or take numerous places to pay for the lifestyle they desire. Individuals tend to change careers many times during their lives, or so the gig market could be regarded as a manifestation of this happening on a big scale.

Criticisms Of this Gig Economy

Despite its advantages, there are a number of drawbacks to the gig market. While not all companies lean toward hiring contracted workers, the gig market tendency can make it tougher for full-time workers to grow fully in their professions since temporary workers tend to be cheaper to employ and more elastic in their accessibility. Employees who prefer a conventional career route and the security and stability that come with it are being busy out in certain sectors.

For Some employees, the flexibility of functioning gigs can interrupt work-life equilibrium, sleep routines, and actions of everyday life. Flexibility at a gig market often means that employees must make themselves accessible any time gigs develop, irrespective of their other requirements, and has to always be on the search for another gig.

In Effect, employees in a gig market are more similar to entrepreneurs compared to conventional employees. Even though this might mean increased freedom of choice to the individual employee, in addition, it suggests the safety of a stable job with regular pay, rewards, along with a daily routine which have distinguished work for generations are quickly becoming a thing of the past. Additionally, it suggests that employees are taking upon themselves a far bigger share of their market risk of financial ups and downs, changing trends, and unpredictable customer tastes, which have been traditionally borne by Hispanic small business owners that used wage and salaried workers. The lifestyle and exposure to danger that include being a entrepreneur or freelancer might just not be for everybody.

Finally, Due to the fluid nature of gig market trades and relationships, longterm relationships involving employees, employers, customers, and sellers can often erode. This may eliminate the advantages that flow from developing long-term confidence, habitual practice, and familiarity with customers and companies. It might also discourage investment from relationship-specific resources which would otherwise be rewarding to pursue, because no party has an incentive to invest in appreciably within a connection which just lasts until the second gig comes along.

Who's Part of the New Gig Economy?

1. TECHNOLOGY PLATFORM COMPANIES

· Technology platform businesses have been a significant force in the growth of their gig market. Included in this class are companies like Uber, Lyft, Airbnb, Etsy, TaskRabbit and othershnology platf

· These platform companies have a couple different commonalities:

1. Facilitate direct trades between customer and manufacturer.

2. Flexible work schedules for gig employees.

3. Online payments, where platforms require a cut.

4. Online reviews and profiles of both manufacturers and customers.

2. GIG WORKERS

· Gig works could be classified into two broad classes:

1. Labor suppliers

O For instance—Motorists, handymen, delivery guys

o Lower-income and Less-educated employees who rely on gig job to get their whole livelihood, often because they have difficulty locating other job choices.

2. Goods suppliers

O For instance—Artists, musicians, clothes retailers

o Higher-income and More-educated employees who don't rely on their gig job earnings, frequently because they've another fulltime occupation; their gig job normally supplies supplemental income.

3. CONSUMERS

Resource: Presentation by Ms. Molly Turner in"The Gig Economy: The Rise of the Freelance Workforce" in NACo's 2017 Annual Conference & Exposition at Franklin County, Ohio, July 2017

The Growth of the Gig Economy - Suggestions for Counties

The gig market is a Kind of work that's still mostly undefined and unrecognized by U.S. policy, from the neighborhood up to the national level. Nonetheless, the gig market is growing and affecting how Americans view operate, which introduces a variety of challenges such as counties.

1. SHIFTING MINDSET OF WORK

The Increase of the gig market represents a change from the way Americans view perform. Rather than a more conventional system by which a worker works fulltime for just 1 company, some employees decide to put in the gig market to its flexibility, freedom and personal gratification that it supplies them.4 Dr. Brown clarified to workshop participants who his pupils expressed interest in greater control and freedom over their career courses. His pupils will also be serial multitaskers: most of these need the stability of a single anchor employer, together with the versatility of simultaneous, smaller tasks. They would like to spread their gift among different tasks.

2. POTENTIAL FUTURE WORKFORCE POLICIES

A lot of America's current labour policies and social security Internet were created before in the 20th century using another work culture in your mind. 5 Workers were anticipated, and a lot more probable, to operate at the same company until retirement and get benefits from this corporation. 6 Today, however, counties will need to be well prepared to adapt to the shifting labor agreements. The gig market labour force is freelance and contract-based. Because of this, gig employees, as independent contractors, don't get benefits, such as health insurance, in the technology platform firms; instead, they need to secure them independently.

Throughout the workshop, Ms. Turner clarified a few prospective ideas which are circulating, such as:

"Dependent contractor" as a potential new category of employee to spell out gig employees. Freelancers who get nearly all their earnings from a particular business would fall under this class, and the corporation must supply benefits and follow specific regulations.

Mobile benefits, that can be advantages possessed by workers and taken to every new job they've. Businesses that hire workers as freelancers would lead to these gains based on the prorated quantity of work completed for the provider.

Counties Can adopt the gig market and learn how to exploit the advantages, while also handling the challenges and tumultuous effects associate with this.

1. RECOGNIZE IT

The increase of the gig market is a worldwide trend and this tendency doesn't show signs of slowing. By way of instance, as Hon. Fitzgerald triumphed, individuals are making a living via several resources and utilizing their abilities with various companies. Intuit and Emergent Research predicted that"the variety of folks working on-demand [gig] occupations will increase by 3.9 million Americans in 2016 to 9.2 million by 2021." 7 Hon. Fitzgerald said that counties must realize this change is already occurring and be ready to adapt. County officials may teach their residents about gig job because the legitimate function of a different contractor. Also, as Ms. Turner suggested, counties may create programs to assist employees in the gig market create appropriate budgets so that they could pay taxes at the conclusion of their financial year, and invite them to buy small company licenses when appropriate. Many gig employees may not know their gig job is valid and consequently not pay the right law or procuring a company permit. Counties can improve their earnings by simply describing to their inhabitants that gig function is"work"

2. RECORD AND MEASURE IT

a sizable portion of realizing the gig market and legitimatizing its function entails measuring and recording its scope and effects. Since Ms. Turner proposed, counties could identify important gig market businesses in their regional or local markets and collect input from employees and employers in those industries about the best way best to create county policies and programs which are inclusive of their gig market.

Collecting data on taxpayers involved with the gig market may also help counties create better-targeted policies to function certain constituencies.

Ultimately, Ms. Turner also suggested that counties analyze how big a function the gig market is acting in their markets and examine how they could enhance their policies to encourage positive results, such as raised taxation, use fees or other kinds of potential earnings.

3. ADAPT TO CHANGES

The gig market includes both challenges and benefits. For most employees, the growth of this gig market has provided new sources of earnings and brand new work opportunities. The gig employees, nevertheless, are freelancers with no advantages offered by traditional work arrangements; therefore, they might wind up consuming more county social services.

For counties, a developing gig market might lead to higher economic activity and spending in their own county, possibly raised earnings, use fees or other kinds of earnings. The independent builders part of this gig market are small companies with one worker. As Dr. Brown said, counties may create it as simple and easy as possible to acquire the licenses or permits that they deem necessary. Additionally, counties can market when these procedures become automated or streamlined to encourage gig employees to receive their license.

There continue to be restricted examples of counties cooperating with gig market providers, therefore, as Dr. Brown clarified, it's a fantastic time for counties to experiment and build the finest local solutions. Ms. Turner encouraged businesses to think beyond the box with their policies and reevaluate their definitions of services and work to accommodate all the various sorts of jobs that their citizens may have, and also to make opportunities for economic development in their communities.

Freelancing was a matter for a long time, but in recent years, the Amount of independent contractors has skyrocketed. Whether you have the change to a tumultuous financial climate or philosophical tendencies (milennials put a greater value on flexbile work along with a purposeful work goal than they perform wages, for example), it is apparent that the gig market is here to remain.

Definition of this Gig Economy

The expression"gig market" refers to an overall workforce Atmosphere Where short term engagements, temporary contracts, and independent contracting is trivial. Additionally, it is known as the"freelancer market,""agile work force,""sharing market," or even"independent workforce" You may think that it's a buzzword, and you would be right, but the widespread development of startups behind the gig market (and the amount of employees hammering them) are a certain sign that the essence of function as we know it's changing.

The freelancer market (or freelancer market) differs from Conventional employment because jobs aren't permanent, but specifically, the expression relates to a lot of one-off jobs or person change missions. On the other hand, the expression may also be used to mention longer-term freelancer structures and separate contracting missions.

The Way the Gig Economy Works

Individually, a gig (a single task, mission, or task) Represents a small part of a worker's income. When employees aggregate many different jobs or changes for various customers or businesses, their cumulative earnings may be like that of fulltime occupation. Others leverage short-term gigs as a means to make a part-time income or supplemental income over the side. It functions both ways, together with employees looking for adaptive, short-term working agreements and businesses trying to employ temporary contract employees instead of full-time workers. What's the gig market?

More importantly, the gig market works on tech platforms That aim to link employees searching for flexible work agreements with the firms who want them at a centralized place, including an app or site. Some programs are concentrated on particular markets, such as warehouse and hospitality employees, dog-walking providers, or other special services, while some are wider, linking gig employees with businesses and customers for jobs which range from housekeeping solutions to composing.

At the freelance market, employees operate as independent Contractors, meaning that their customers pay them an agreed-upon speed for services rendered. Within an independent contracting arrangement, employees are responsible for paying and saving their own taxes and are not qualified for the common advantages of fulltime employment like access to group health insurance or retirement investments and savings account. But as a result of the growth of the individual work force, benefits like health insurance policy, independent retirement accounts (IRAs)liability and accident insurance are far somewhat more accessible than previously. Additionally, workers working as independent contractors make to benefit from the tax advantages of managing their own business, such as tax deductions such as non-reimbursed working expenses like travel, supplies, and so on.

Advantages of this Gig Economy

Employees who leverage the freelancer market to make or supplement Their incomes frequently cite flexibility since the largest attraction. When a professional is not dedicated to one employer at a fulltime job arrangement, they keep greater control over their work schedules as a result of the capability to take just the gigs, duties, or shifts which don't interfere with their other obligations.

Members of the work force with full-time professions who Wish to Supplement their earnings can simply pick up a couple of gigs at the evenings or on weekends. Skilled professionals can apply greater control over their career trajectory by participating in projects that are challenging and constructing an impressive resume of outcomes, allowing them to secure higher-level and better-paying fulltime rankings. Many, but simply choose to stay part of the individual workforce as a result of the versatility and earnings potential it gives them.

The Growth of the individual workforce benefits not simply employees But also firms who will reap the cost savings of enlisting short-term support to accommodate demand with no administrative expenses of hiring full-time employees. Businesses are not making employer contributions to retirement savings account, for example, or contributing to the cost of group medical insurance policy for gig employees, so the general price of hiring aid is often less than the price of selecting a full-time worker.

Advantages of independent work

Businesses can quickly leverage proficient professionals for Particular, short-term jobs who'd otherwise be too pricey for a developing business to keep a fulltime staffer. For example, a developing startup might not have the funds to finance a six-figure executive wages, however a five-figure fee to get a three-month consulting involvement could be contained in budget.

Furthermore, it boosts the market at large by creating it Potential to deliver services and goods faster and better. Studies indicate that by the year 2020, 43% of the American workforce will include independent contractors. With digitization and automation threatening some conventional tasks, the freelancer market can offer job protection, but not in the standard sense. While this might seem backward (how do adopting temporary work potentially bring about long-term job safety?) , it pays homage to the thought that you shouldn't place your eggs all in 1 basket; at the independent work force, getting your position downsized does not mean that you've suddenly lost your whole income.

Best Practices for Leveraging the Gig Economy

It is easier than ever for businesses in practically every business To leverage the gig market, and employees with many different abilities at all levels Can easily secure short-term gigs to make a living or supplement an existing Income, especially in case you observe some best practices:

Find your specialty. Use your Present abilities and interests, however, Additionally follow your passions.

Leverage technology systems. As Soon as You've identified your attention (the kind of job you are interested in and qualified for), subscribe to tech platforms that connect employees with your abilities to the businesses who want them. These programs make it simple to secure temporary function with no time-consuming job of looking for customers by yourself and advertising your services.

Establish your own schedule. While among the biggest benefits of this gig Market is flexibility, so determining your accessibility beforehand makes it much easier to weed out gigs that make use of your program and lowers the probability you'll have to make adjustments or bow from a previously-accepted gig.

Manage your own finances. As an independent employee, developing a Budget and organizing your financing is essential. Determine how much you will want to put aside for taxation and produce a method for documenting your expenses and income. Tax time will be less stressful, along with your tax preparer will thank you.

Heal every gig as though it's an audition. Give each job your all—even if you are working a single change for a provider. Some on-demand staffing programs have company feedback loops, permitting businesses to rate and examine temporary employees, which may significantly affect your ability to secure future work. Even if there is no formal inspection mechanism in place, your reputation is essential to your own success, and surpassing expectations may make you recommendations and referrals.

The gig market provides plentiful opportunities for your workforce And companies alike. The development of the individual work force is here to stay, because of technology advancements which make it simpler than ever for employees to find temporary jobs that afford them the flexibility and freedom they desire.

CHAPTER TWO:
THRIVING IN THE GIG ECONOMY

"Perhaps you have been on a trapeze?" That is Just how Martha, an independent adviser, responded when we asked her to explain her work at the five years since she had left a international consulting company to embark by herself. She'd lately attempted the artwork, which she viewed as a fantastic metaphor for her entire life: the emptiness she felt between duties; the exhilaration of landing another engagement; the subject, concentration, and elegance that mastering her livelihood required. Trapeze artists appear to take enormous risks, she clarified, but a security system—such as nets, gear, and fellow actors—supports them"They seem to be in their own, however they are not."

Martha (whose name, like other people in this Guide, was altered) is Portion of a burgeoning part of the workforce broadly referred to as the gig market. Approximately 150 million employees in North America and Western Europe have abandoned the comparatively stable boundaries of organizational life—sometimes by choice, sometimes not—to function as independent contractors. A number of this expansion reflects the development of ride-hailing and task-oriented support platforms, however a current report from McKinsey discovered that knowledge-intensive businesses and creative jobs are the greatest and weakest parts of the freelance market.

To learn exactly what it takes to be Prosperous in separate function, we recently Finished an detailed study of 65 gig employees. We discovered unusually similar sentiments over generations and jobs: Each of people we surveyed acknowledged they felt a plethora of private, societal, and financial anxieties with no cover and assistance of a conventional company—but they also promised that their liberty was a decision and they wouldn't give up the advantages which came with it. Though they concerned about unpredictable programs and financing, they felt they'd mustered more guts and were major richer lifestyles than their corporate counterparts.

We found that the Best independent employees navigate this Tension with common plans. They cultivate four kinds of relations—to set, patterns, goal, and individuals—which help them suffer the psychological ups and downs of the work and gain power and inspiration from their own liberty. Since the gig market grows globally, these plans are becoming more and more relevant. Really, we think they might also be very helpful to any corporate workers that are working more inexpensively, in the home or a remote officeor who believe that they may one day want—or want—to leap right into an independent career.

Independent employees create a"holding environment" for their work.

Create or Perish

First thing we understood once we started interviewing independent Advisers and musicians was that the bets of both independent work are high—not only financially but also existentially. Unshackled from supervisors and company standards, individuals are able to select assignments which get the most out of their abilities and reflect their own true interests. They feel ownership over what they create and within their whole lives. 1 study manager told me,"I could be the most I have ever been in almost any job."

However, the Purchase Price of these liberty is a precariousness that looks to not subside over time. The strongest, well-established individuals we interviewed still fret about money and standing and at times believe that their identity is at stake. You can not keep calling yourself a consultant, as an instance, if customers stop requesting your services. A well-published author told us"You become your job. Should you write a fantastic book...it is truly great, and if you do not achieve it, then you need to take...that collapse could define that which you are yourself" A artist agreed:"There is no coming. That is a fantasy."

Because of This, productivity is an extreme preoccupation for Everybody we interviewed. It supplies self-expression and also an antidote to precariousness. Interestingly, but the folks we spoke with are not simply focusing on getting things completed and marketed. They take care of being in the office—with the discipline to frequently generate services or products which locate a marketplace—and now being in their job: with the guts to remain fully invested in the process and outcome of the labour.

Maintaining productivity is a continuous battle. Distress and Distractions can hamper this, and the two impediments abound in people's lives. 1 executive mentor gave a poignant description of a unproductive day:"It is when there is so much to accomplish that I am disorganized and can not get my act together. [In the day,] the very same e-mails I opened at the morning continue to be available. The files that I wanted to have done aren't done. I got distracted and feel as though I wasted time" A day such as this, he saidleaves him total of self-doubt.

After we asked interviewees that the secret to getting through these times and Ultimately modulates productivity as they explained, we found that a paradox at the center of their responses. All of them wish to preserve their liberty and, oftentimes, their unsettledness (which consultant described as the secret to continuing learning and"keeping my advantage"), but they also devote a wonderful deal of time creating a"holding environment"—a physiological, societal, and emotional space for their job.

This notion—initially used by the British psychoanalyst Donald Winnicott To explain how careful caregivers ease children's growth by buffering them from distress and creating space for experimentation—has been used in the area of adult development to refer to states where people are their best and develop. Corporate workers, naturally, can locate them using a fantastic boss in a good business. However, for independent workers, a holding environment is not a talent than an achievement; it has to be cultivated, and it could be lost.

So they make these surroundings for themselves by setting and Maintaining that which we call"liberating connections"—since they free up people to be independently creative and bind them to function to ensure their output does not wane.

The Four Connections

Area.

Disconnected in the corporate office, the more people we interviewed locate Areas to work that shield them from external distractions and anxieties and let them prevent feeling rootless. Though many maintained their work was mobile, they still looked to have somewhere to escape. 1 author told us"People fail because they do not create a time and space to perform whatever it is that they have to do."

We seen many of those spaces in person and noticed several Similarities. They feel restricted—almost uncomfortably so in the instance of a few artists. They're used consistently for many work. They permit easy access to the instruments of this operator's trade and also to little else. And they are devoted to work; folks usually leave them after their everyday tasks are finished. 1 software engineer, whose house office includes all these attributes, explained it as a"fighter pilot cockpit," where every thing he desires is within arm's reach. "Sometimes it is amazing," he said, but"when I am there, the open area is in my head"

Despite these commonalities, every workspace can also be exceptional, with a Place, furniture, supplies, and decorations that reflect the idiosyncrasy of its proprietor work. These areas aren't solely protective cocoons for your functioning self—they provoke that, too. Karla, an independent adviser who originally told us she can do work"where I appear and'm doing something which has positive effect on earth," eventually confessed her house office is where she moves to prevent diversion and find inspiration, literally surrounded with her present and possible projects, organized in observable and accessible piles. "When I walk through this door, I step to an area that embraces all of the various elements of myself," she informed me. "I'm at home in there." Without that location and the distance it provides her, Karla clarified, she'd most likely be overly sensitive to outside requirements and thus less concentrated and free.

Routines.

In organizations, patterns are often associated with security or dull bureaucracy. But a developing body of study has proven that elite athletes, scientific geniuses, artists that are popular, as well as regular employees use patterns to increase performance and focus. The professionals we talked with are inclined to rely on these at precisely the exact same manner.

Some patterns enhance people's workflow: maintaining a schedule; after a To-do listing; starting the afternoon with the most hard job or using a customer call; leaving a sentence incomplete within an unfinished manuscript to produce a simple start another day; crossing the studio floor whilst reflecting on a fresh slice. Other patterns, usually involving meditation, sleep, nutrition, or exercise, include private maintenance into people's lives. Both types frequently have a ritual component which enriches people's sense of control and order in uncertain conditions.

1 adviser we interviewed requires a bath each morning and visualizes What she would like to achieve while she awakens. Another adviser, Matthew, that specializes in assisting boards concentrate on creation, keeps a rigorous daily program:"I am up at 6:00 and there is exercise. I package my own spouse's lunch. We beg. She is outside the door about 8:00. I am in my office by 8:30, and that I really do work in which there is deeper idea required—writing or design—in the daytime. That is when I am at my best. In the afternoon I program telephone calls, a lot of the company or financial things which will need to get carried out." This subject extends into his wardrobe:"I constantly get dressed to the workplace. Many days in summer that I wear shorts when I am not on the street, but I shave and shower as though I was moving to a office different from house."

That may sound stiff, but it will help Matthew pour himself in his job. He along with other successful independent employees appear to follow the recommendation of the French novelist Gustave Flaubert:"Be regular and orderly in your life...so that you might be violent and original in your work"

Goal.

For many individuals in our analysis, striking out in their originally Involved doing anything work would permit them to locate a footing on the industry. Nevertheless, they were determined that achievement means taking just work that obviously connects into a wider purpose. All could articulate why their job, or their very best work—make it enable girls through movie, expose dangerous marketing techniques, sustain the American folk music heritage, or assist corporate leaders triumph with ethics—is greater than a way of making a living.

Goal produces a bridge between their private interests and motives and a demand on earth. Matthew, by way of instance, stated that although initially he believed"a certain desperation around getting customers and earning an income" over time his perspective of achievement altered"to one that's a whole lot about living a lifetime of service to other people and making the world a better place"

An executive coach we now Interviewed told me that purpose retains her steady, motivated, and inspiring. "A large distinction between powerful independents as well as also the individuals that aren't or return [to corporate tasks] is getting to this place of understanding what you are supposed to do. This provides me elegance for those ups and downs. It gives me the power to decline work which is not in alignment. It provides me a quality of credibility and assurance that customers are attracted to. It is useful to constructing or maintaining the company and serving the folks I'm here to serve."

We discovered that purpose, Similar to the other relations, the two binds and frees individuals by orienting and bettering their job.

Folks.

Humans are social animals. Studies in corporate configurations have long Demonstrated how important other men and women are to our professions—as role models who show us that we may turn into, and as coworkers that help us advancement from sharing our route. Researchers also have cautioned about a "loneliness epidemic" hitting on the office, which independent employees can surely be at even higher risk.

However, people who interviewed are aware of the dangers of societal Isolation and try to prevent it. Although many are ambivalent about formal peer classes, which they frequently see as insipid replacements for collegiality, all reported with individuals they turn to for encouragement and reassurance. Occasionally these are direct function models or encouraging collaborators; in some other instances they are relatives, friends, or connections in similar areas, who can not always offer you specific work guidance but help our research participants push through hard times and embolden them to carry the dangers their job involves.

Success at the gig market comes from a balance between Viability and energy.

Matthew, by Way of Example, noticed that reaching out to individuals in his internal Circle helps calm his nervousness "If I had been left in my, I could sit in the office and move down a rat hole. You are left to your own internal voice, and it spirals into ruminating." Karla told me that she, also, frequently turns to a couple of peers with whom she is close. "All of the work I do from the independent market comes through those links," she explained. However, their aid goes beyond referrals. "My capacity to process, grow, and develop as a human being and know that I'm at the job I am doing comes in the discussions that I have with those people," she clarified. "These individuals are how I understand what I am supposed to do."

Redefining Success

In popular direction stories, career success generally includes safety and equanimity. For independent employees, however, both are ultimately elusive. And most of the people surveyed informed us they believe powerful.

Most we spoke to think they would not Have the Ability to find the Identical psychological Strength or space in a conventional workplace. Martha, the adviser who compared herself into a trapeze performer, remembered that she became"more powerful professionally" and"more comfy in my individuality " if a trusted counselor helped her reframe—and possess—her battle, rather than seek ways to prevent it. "She helped me know that I could think of myselfwhich I do, as a pioneer. I really don't fit in any classes which exist in organizations, and it is more effective for me personally to be independent" This way, uncertainty and distress weren't only tolerable but affirming—signals that she was where she had to be.

When we talked, she depicted employment as no more an anchor she Missed however a shackle she had been blessed enough to split. "I really don't know I would framework [my life] because precariousness anymore," she reasoned. "I'd frame it really living."

CHAPTER THREE:
FREELANCE ECONOMY

The freelance market, too Called the gig market , is a labour market comprising a rising amount of short-term contracts. Businesses hire self-employed employees to tackle certain work in return for an allowable payment, instead of supplying them permanent places.

Freelancers would be the people who make themselves available to be hired for such temporary function. They may find tasks through classified advertisements, temporary staffing agencies, or alternative ways.

KEY TAKEAWAYS

- The freelancer market, also referred to as the gig market, revolves round hiring self-employed employees to tackle certain work in return for an allowable payment.
- An uncertain financial climate, need for more flexible working hours, and price advantages for corporations and technological improvements have prompted the amount of individuals working as freelancers to innovate the past few decades.
- Advantages of working freelancer include flexible hours, the option to work at home, and also the chance to deduct business expenses from earnings.
- Drawbacks include being responsible for paying taxes rather than getting the a number of different advantages that accompany permanent employment.
- Knowing the Freelance Economy
- Freelancing isn't a new phenomenon. Independent Builders have been in existence for decades. In the last few decades, the amount of these has skyrocketed in areas as diverse as commercial design, resort management (like Airbnb), and cab driving, through ridesharing programs like Lyft Inc. (LYFT) and Uber Technologies Inc. (UBER).

The change toward self-employment can result from a number of things, such as an unclear economic climate, need for more flexible working hours, cost-savings for businesses, and digitalization—that the world wide web has made it considerably easier for individuals to operate remotely.

Half of America's work force is Anticipated to go freelancer within the next ten years, up from 35 percent in 2018.

The way the Freelance Economy Works

Freelancers can work as many hours as they like. Some work Fulltime, balancing a range of different tasks for a variety of customers or businesses. Others do it on a part time foundation, permitting them to earn a little additional income on the side.

Freelancers usually agree on a commission upfront with customers and then, oftentimes, normally send them an bill once the job is complete in order to be compensated.

Unlike permanent employees, freelancers are believed Independent contractors. That means that they are responsible for paying their particular taxation , medical insurance policy , and retirement gifts . In addition they aren't eligible for holiday benefits or sick leave.

Benefits of this Freelance Economy

The freelance market has given many people the chance To pursue livelihoods which were previously tough to enter. By way of instance, before a cab driver in several cities needed to buy or rent a costly medallion, in effect a limited license to run a taxi. Nowadays drivers require just a vehicle and a smartphone.

Working freelancer also offers flexible hours and the Opportunity to Work at home. Another advantage for freelancers is they can subtract company expenses in their earnings, reducing the quantity of taxable revenue they cover.

In 2018, almost 57 million Americans worked freelance, according to a poll by Upwork and Freelancers Union, representing over 35 percent of the whole workforce.

Criticisms of those Freelance Economy

The freelance market has been blamed for a host of new social problems. Freelance employees in the U.S. don't get company health insurance, forcing them to purchase expensive individual coverages, nor holiday benefits or sick leave; a disorder that prevents work can lead to severe fiscal strain.

Freelancers additionally cover hefty self-employment Taxes and don't become matching retirement savings gains. Because of this, many fiscal planners fear that the current freelance employees won't have sufficient retirement savings to approximate their existing standard of living in older age.

Past the private Financial consequences of freelancer employment, the freelancer market has led to a bunch of bigger problems. By way of instance, Airbnb has directed many home owners to currently let their distances to short-term traffic. They've in effect changed from being landlords to freelancer resort operators, alerting housing shortages, in addition to a increase in nuisance complaints from neighbors and also worries regarding criminal activity.

Similarly, the widespread prevalence of ridesharing was Dampened by reports of juvenile motorists attacking passengers. Where previously some businesses were viewed as being over-regulated, a concern with all the freelancer market is too little oversight. Society continues to grapple with the ideal balance between these variables.

The Growth of the freelancer market has also taken a toll on American salaries, that are stagnant for decades, and the general fulltime job marketplace as more companies change tasks to domestic freelancers or abroad.

Special Considerations

Businesses generally gain from hiring independent contractors. They cover them for the job they do but aren't required to provide them some of the expensive advantages they are obligated to supply permanent workers with.

The federal government and Several states impose severe penalties On businesses which re-classify full-time workers as freelancer"advisers" Normally, valid freelancers must operate from an off-site place, have multiple customers, rather than be a current employee of the company.

WHAT IS FREELANCING?

A Freelancer, or independent contractor, is a self employed person who does not need to commit to one, long-term employer. Rather, they operate independently for many unique businesses or customers. Freelancers normally charge by the hour or day and aren't required to enroll as a company if they function under their own name.

It is Often thought the expression meaning that a freelancer was utilized in Sir Walter Scott's classic Ivanhoe (1820), where Scott said,"I provided Richard the support of my Free Lances, and he also denied themI will lead them to Hull, grab on transport, and embark for Flanders; thanks to this bustling times, a person of activity will always find employment" To put it differently, those persons were mercenary's who supplied their services to the maximum bidder.

But, There was a previous instance of this word at 1809 by Thomas N. Brown's, The Life and Times of Hugh Miller by saying,"But if the battle was hottest, Hugh Miller was a faithful combatant, not even a free lance."

Today, The expression is frequently connected with photographers, writers, editors, developers, site designers, and specialist advisors, in addition to several other specialist services.

According To Forbes, the very best freelancing gigs are:

Marketing - Job supervisors, Marketing coordinators, or Marketing Managers can earn between $46 to $52 an hour.

Business Project Management - Project Manager, Process Analyst are Estimated to create $34 to $46 an hour.

Internet Development - Developing, testing, or supplying Support for applications or programs may lead to earnings of $36 to $43 an hour.

Composing - Bloggers, copy editors, and content managers may create $25 to $30 an hour, Making freelance composing a profitable option for wordsmiths

Accounting - It is estimated that freelance accountants can earn between $16 to $30 an hour.

Insurance Inspection - Collecting information, for example Photos, and composing insurance reports can make roughly $28 per hour.

Teaching/Tutoring - Educating online courses or being a Tutor can earn $20 to $28 an hour.

Social Media - Being a neighborhood supervisor or societal networking coordinators Can bring about $20 to $25 a hour.

Graphic Design - Site and program designers are Able to make approximately $21+ per hour.

Administrative Assistant - Expert assistants can earn between $17 to $20 an hour.

PROS AND CONS OF FREELANCING

Whether You have been laid-off, your tired of the daily grind, or you only wish to go into business on your own, starting an independent company delivers numerous amazing benefits that many companies just can not compete with.

Benefits Of Freelance Work

The Experts of becoming an independent contractor include:

You are the Boss - This means That You Could select when And in which you work. If you are a night owl, you are able to work the whole night and sleep until noon without having to leave the home. Also, you could even choose what jobs you wish to perform on. If you are a photographer, you might fear working weddings. This usually means you don't need to take a wedding job if you don't need to, but you are going to have the ability to pick just the events or scenarios which you would rather shoot pictures of.

You May Earn More Cash - If You've Got the drive, salespeople Have the capability to earn more cash than the ordinary individual. Some reports have found that freelancers really earn 45 percent more than the typical full-time worker.

Reduced waiver - Federal and state taxes Aren't withheld from your Paychecks and salespeople cover the IRS right four occasions each year, for instance, self-employed taxation set of social security. In addition they have access to tax deductions such as travel, office, meal, and online expenses.

Work-Life Balance - Between flexible programs, as well as the Fact that only 29 percent of freelance employees put in over 40 hours each week, franchisees possess an amazing work life balance.

Happier, Healthier - Research have found that freelancers Are happier and healthier, both mentally and emotionally, compared to conventional employees.

The Benefits of Freelance Work

Even though There are numerous amazing benefits surrounding freelancer work, there are a few disadvantages which needs to be considered.

No Job Security - If your customers do not have any work For you, you then can not earn any money. Even if you're a worker, you can always have work to finish unless your company goes out of business or you are laid off.

Inconsistent Work - There are months when there's a slew of Work to finish and the paychecks are greater than you predicted. On the other hand, the job may dry up and the next month you are just making half of everything you created the prior month. As a worker, at least you know how much you are paycheck will be every month so you can budget accordingly.

There Are No Benefits - Some of the benefits of working for Somebody else is the employer will deal with all your wellbeing or retirement bonuses or benefits such as paid holidays or gain sharing. Purchasing your health insurance is frequently more costly than what can be obtained from a company.

You Need to Take Care of Accounting - Taxes, accounting, paying invoices, and Managing cash flow is your decision. Even though there's readily available applications to aid you with your bookkeeping, it is an extra job that conventional workers don't need to worry with.

You Risk Not Getting Paid - It is Not Unusual for independent Contractors to have trouble getting compensated for their solutions. Some customers either do not pay heed or they do not pay in any way. Unlike conventional workers where you constantly know that a paycheck will soon arrive.

You Have to Have the Ability to inspire yourself without prodding in the outside source.

SETTING UP YOUR WORKPLACE

After Weighing the advantages and disadvantages of freelancing, you might have determined that you are going to proceed and become an independent contractor. Now it is time to receive your office figured out so you can start working.

If You myself, you are already at an edge. You could just sit in the kitchen table or convert this spare space into a workplace and not need to worry with becoming distracted by other people. If you reside with other people, you are going to need to discover a space where you could be left during"work hours" Preferably this distance, are an area where there is a door that closes.

If Your house is not conducive to freelancing, then look at setting up shop in a neighborhood coffee shop or leasing out a Setting Up Your Workplace commercial office area. In reality, you might have the ability to hunt for co-office distances through websites like ShareDesk or even PivotDesk if you simply want something temporarily or in an adequate cost. The library is a superb place to get some peace and quiet to operate in.

No Matter in which you choose to produce your office, ensure it's at a place that's free of distractions and also matches your requirements. A writer only wants their notebook and a socket to charge battery. However, a photographer might require a darkroom to develop their pictures, in addition to an area to edit the photographs.

BRANDING YOURSELF

Whether You opt to go only by your title,"Jane Smith Writer," or integrating a Business title,"Elite Website Design," you need to create a brand on your own. Apart from your business name, you should also have a symbol Which Can Be put Across multiple mediums. Should you make use of your name, your logo could only function as the Initials within an exceptional font which would be set on your site, social media Accounts, and bills. If You Are Thinking about business cards, there are 100 Business cards in Vistaprint for only $7.99. You should also have a committed Company telephone number and address, even if it is a P.O. box, to add to a professional brand.

Most Importantly, you have to get a site where you can showcase your portfolio, discuss testimonials, and encourage Branding Yourself your providers. In regards to your site, ensure the domain name is easy to remember (your title would be the simplest place to begin) easy to describe, and explains what you're doing. By way of instance, if your name is John Doe and you are a social networking supervisor, perhaps you could put money into the domain "socialmediajohn.com."

Your Site should also contain these elements:

- An announcement which introduces yourself to potential customers, such as qualifications and education.
- Describe the services which you offer.
- Display examples of your job.
- Contact details such as address, contact number, and email address.
- Branding Yourself makes it much easier for you to stick out from other freelancers on your area, showcase your professionalism, and provides you with the chance to properly market your services and locate more freelance projects.

CREATING YOUR PORTFOLIO

As Previously mentioned, developing a professional portfolio is a significant part of your website as it highlights your abilities and abilities. Bear in mind, a portfolio is an efficient method to entice customers as it sets their mind at ease when they could see for themselves that you're more than capable of tackling the job at hand.

When Building your portfolio, keep the following in mind:

Just demonstrate the jobs that you are most proud of and think that reflects your very best work.

Prove diversity in your job. If you are a writer, by way of instance, provide examples of posts that discuss different topics to reveal your diversity.

Include your contact info so it makes it simpler for customers to get in contact with you.

Regardless In case you've got a decade worth of job, or are only beginning, a portfolio is a significant assist for salespeople. And, here several advocated hosts and sites that could certainly help you make and discuss your online portfolio.

Carbonmade - With plans starting at only $6/month, Carbonmade lets Freelancers in many different areas to easily customize their portfolios using a private domainname.

Portfoliobox - There's a free version or compensated Pro-edition for Portfolio that permits artists, architects, designers, and stylists to discuss their work using their very own domainnames.

Behance - As Part of Adobe's Creative Cloud service it is Extremely simple to upload your own work on Behance. Why is Behance stand out is that there is a project board and hunt choice for companies searching for creatives.

Squarespace - Together with the capability to synch to societal media stations and Analytics accounts, Squarespace is a potent option in regards to sharing your finest imaginative work. THE

Journo Portfolio - This really is an Superb online portfolio For writers and journalists.

WordPress - although not just a portfolio site, WordPress is indeed Flexible and flexible you could turn it into any kind of site which you may consider.

SETTING ESTIMATES AND RATES

One Of the toughest parts about being a freelancer is deciding the prices you'll bill for the services. If you charge too little, you rush into the probability of being handed over because might see you as an amateur - not to mention you might not have the ability to generate a suitable living. If you charge a lot, you are going to lose out on a work opportunity because the customer can find somebody else that will do the work as well because you personally but in a fraction of the purchase price.

Estimates vs. Quotes

When Being approached by a potential customer, it is common practice for them to request a quote or speed. The gap between both is fairly straightforward to describe. Setting Fees and Estimates

An Quote is generally a demanding cost of exactly what the job will cost the company. While a quote is not a fixed article, it is typically within 20 percent of the final price. A quotation differs from quotes because usually a quotation is going to wind up being the closing fixed sum of this undertaking.

With Software from websites such as Due.com, it is possible to send an itemized breakdown of solutions as a quotation or quote to prospective customers so they have a better knowledge of the expenses involved with the project and your own services.

How To ascertain the purchase price of Your Services

There Are three distinct approaches to use when deciding how much you are likely to bill for your services. These include:

Price Plus Pricing

This Is a favorite, and relatively simple method in figuring out just how much to bill. You just decide the costs involved in creating a solution and then adding a little something extra into that amount so which you may turn a profit. This is particularly useful for salespeople such as photographers, videographers, and musicians since they know just how much it costs to development and materials. Consequently, they'd take those prices and put in their own desired profit margin to think of the speed.

For Independent contractors such as authors and freelance web designers, so this might be a bit more challenging to determine. The ideal way to settle a speed is by understanding how much your monthly expenditures are - food, online, insurance - then add just how much is necessary for gain to cover your own expenses.

Economy Rate Pricing

This Is another powerful, and convenient method of figuring out your own rates. By researching how much different salespeople in your business are charging for their solutions it provides you a rough estimate of everything, and the best way to bill customers. Maybe you thought $20 a hour was reasonable for the web development skills, but understood that additional specialists were charging for the whole project, which might come out to $25 a hour when broken down. It is possible to go to freelancer sites such as Upwork or even Elance to scoop out what competitors are charging. You might even see Coroflot's Design Salary Guide as a starting point to compare prices.

Maintain In your mind though that place has a significant effect on market prices. By way of instance, a writer at the Philippines or India will charge less money a writer in New York or San Francisco since the price of living is more expensive in North America. Even though this can lead to some issues, most customers do prefer working with customers in their portion of the Earth, so know about the rates that applicable contractors in your area are charging.

Worth Driven Pricing

If You are a graphic designer could you expect to bill, and get, the exact same speed from a Fortune 500 company and a neighborhood coffee shop?

Absolutely not. And, that is basically what worth pushed pricing is. To put it differently, the customer pays for what they think the service is worth. But, you also need to ensure you live up to expectations.

When Employing this technique, you are able to start off using a flat rate. Let us say that you are a graphic designer and you charge $1,000 to get work. It's possible to charge extra to your add-ons the customer requests because the neighborhood coffee shop may well not require the excess add-ons the Fortune 500 business does.

Discovering Your Cost Structure

Even though The strategies listed below are a excellent place to begin determining how much your services will cost a customer, you still need to settle on a cost structure to start a successful freelance career.

Hourly Rate

This Is popular rate structure utilized by salespeople in which you keep track of the hours it can take to finish a job for a customer and charge them for all those hours. To Work out How much to charge per hour, answer these questions:

Just how much do other people charge? If the business standard is 30 per hour and You are charging $100 per hourthen you might want to reevaluate your own rate.

What is the maximum amount you may charge? This may require a Little trial and error, however when your services are actually worth $100 a hour and you've got customers ready to pay that speed, then that is just how much you need to charge.

What do you have to survive? Learn just how many billable hours you Can really work a week and calculate your own costs - rent, grocery store, web, insurance, power, and some other statements that are essential. Should you decide you could get the job done about 80 hours a month - that is 20 hours a week and you monthly invoices come out to $2,000, then you have to charge $25 per hour.

One Among the largest problems with hourly prices is that you aren't likely to be in a position to really work 40 hours a week for a job freelancer as you have errands, bookkeeping, and advertising your services in addition to your job. Thus, don't kid yourself into believing that you are likely to earn more money per month than you really will.

Another Issue with hourly prices is you need to keep an eye on time. Can you charge whenever you've got an idea whilst driving? And, what is the perfect method to monitor those billable hours? Luckily, websites like Due.com have strong time tracking software which makes this a little simpler.

Daily/Weekly Rates

Rather Of an hourly fee, perhaps you wish to bill your customer through the day or week. This may be successful for a few reasons. For starters, your services might only be necessary for a only a few days or for a week. This usually means you could plan accordingly and funding according to this speed - it is also rather simple to track. $25 days 10 hours is much easier to monitor than only a flat rate of $500 for the week. Clients also enjoy this speed as it pretty much guarantees you'll be focused solely in their job.

Fixed Fate

Another Average rate structure is charging per job. As an instance, you're freelance marketer that charges $1,500 a month for customer jobs. Clients enjoy this arrangement as they're well aware upfront of the expense of this undertaking. And, in addition, it makes your life simpler since you do not need to do a lot of budgeting and monitoring.

When Moving this route, be certain you are aware of how long and effort a job will require you to finish before sending out a quote. The very last thing you need is to invest additional time on a project, not get paid a fair speed for the job since the occupation took five times more than you'd calculated it would require.

When Beginning as a freelancer, then it could be okay to undercharge a little. Bear in mind, clients need a bargain and you may use the job to construct your portfolio and have your customers spread the word on how amazing you're. As soon as you get settled, however, you have to get a suitable speed. Just remember you might wish to still bill those first customers of yours somewhat less because they're the individuals who helped establish your freelance career. Consider it a family and friends reduction.

MARKETING AND PROMOTION

If You believed it was hard trying to ascertain your prices as a freelancer, then simply wait till you start attempting to advertise and market your brandnew. Even though this might not be a significant concern for a experienced freelancer or possibly a marketing wiz, it is still a barrier that every freelancer needs to deal if they wish to create a profession of out their individual work.

Earlier It had been mentioned that salespeople need to have a site which introduces themselvesshowcases their job, and contains contact info. A site is an excellent starting point when starting to publicize your brand. And, among the best methods of getting visitors to go to your site is by generating top-notch content your particular audience cares about.

Let us State that you are a freelance accountant. Perhaps you could produce content that helps small business owners with tax queries by writing detailed posts in your site, hosting a podcast or webinar, or producing a infographic that depicts different tax amounts. The notion is that content wouldn't just assist small business owners with earnings, the content demonstrates that you are an expert in the business and also will be shared by other people in the bookkeeping in their sites or social networking reports. To put it differently, you'd do a few excellent ole-fashioned content advertising.

Additional Techniques to get your name on the market is to try out a number of these approaches:

Produce Case studies which do not just illustrate your abilities and abilities, but the way you helped previous customers solve an issue. In case you've got a portfolio on your website, this content is currently up and running.

Request Previous clients if they're eager to offer a testimonial which explains your job and place which testimonial on your site.

Network In-person at business events, the regional chamber of trade, or simply by interacting with relevant groups and forums online. As an instance, you can answer inquiries on Quora or swap ideas with a related LinkedIn group.

Become A guest author for a respected business books or website in your area. Not only will you illustrate your own comprehension, you will also get some traffic that is valuable.

Educate Others in your business by teaching a workshop or class, talking at an event, providing a demonstration, judging a contest, or composing an eBook.

Get Recorded in neighborhood company directories and on both the Google and Facebook advertisements.

Boost Your brand-new swag: t-shirts, pens, coffee mugs, or anything cool things you will think your customers will enjoy.

Offer A totally free consultation, 30-day free trial, or merchandise. Who does not love free stuff?

Freelancers Mostly do a small cold e-mailing. It might be a bit embarrassing at first, and it might not be the best, but it is an essential evil. Just look for the titles of approximately 5-15 potential customers that you would wish to work for, do a little digging, and discover ways to assist them. Then reach out to them via an email. You might need to submit an email type or message Facebook if you can not track down an email address.

Bear in Mind, Cold emails will need to get directly to the stage. Introduce yourself, briefly explain why you are calling themand supply a link that shows your job.

Even though A number of the aforementioned strategies can be powerful, there is nothing as powerful as using your existing network or seeking word-of-mouth referrals. When it is a relative, friend, former co-worker, a college professor, or even previous customer, word-of-mouth recommendations are priceless. You are able to make this coveted recommendation by notifying your present network of friends, family and business partners what you are up to - ideally they will spread the word for you - and by supplying quality work , there'll be customers that'll be pleased to advise you for use other people at the area you're working in.

WHERE TO FIND WORK

Apart from Marketing yourself through articles, using your existing connections, and cold-emailing prospective customers, where else could freelancers land a gig?

Job Boards and Freelance Websites

If You are just beginning, you might not have that big of a community. That is okay since there are tons of job boards and sites out there designed especially to help freelancers find work. Some of the well-known job boards and freelance sites include:

"

Freelancing Is not necessarily as with other companies where there is always the fear that the contest. Freelancing adopts more of a neighborhood vibe. And, that is the reason it is possible to link with other freelancers in your area. Not only are you able to find their guidance, they are throw you a gig here and there when they can not deal with the workload.

You Can socialize with fellow salespeople by connecting online forums such as The Freelance Forum, Work At Home Forum, TalkFreelance, or even by looking for business certain forums such as salespeople. Additionally, the majority of the sites listed above have forums that you associate with other freelancers.

Function To get a Non-Profit

Working For free is an excellent way to construct your portfolio, jumpstart your freelance career, and curiosity prospective customers into providing your services a opportunity. However if you are prepared to give away your services at no cost, why don't you put them to good use by helping a nonprofit? By way of instance, you may use your coding abilities to construct a mobile program for a nonprofit. Does this increase a portfolio, but the board of supervisors for the non-profit might be impressed with your abilities and employ you for another occupation.

Remember. . .Stick To Present Contacts, Media Opportunities, and Promotion

Preventing A freelancing job might take just a little effort on your end initially. However, there are far more than enough freelancing sites and communities accessible which will get your foot in the doorway. What's more, there's nothing wrong with tapping into your current network of connections and media both offline and online to snag a customer.

If You would like to attract new customers, you need to do something casual that catches their attention - if that is an wonderful blog article, guest composing, giving away something at no cost, or cold-emailing companies. Until you've got a steady number of customers, you need to go to wherever the job is.

WORKING WITH CLIENTS

Without Customers your freelance business isn't going anywhere. And as you will encounter great customers who you might even think about a friend, you will also need to manage those customers who you wish you never fulfilled. No matter of that end of the spectrum you are addressing, working with customers is vital. And, here are the very best methods to utilize them so your experience is going to be as simple as possible.

Be On the exact same Page

That May seem obvious, but if working with a customer both parties will need to be on precisely the exact same page. This starts during the pitch period by being mindful of what precisely the customer is trying to find. If you are unclear about what the customer is searching for, do not be afraid to ask question. It is not fun working on a job, turning it , and with the customer reject it as you misunderstood what they had been anticipating.

Especially, You and your customer both have to agree on significant elements of a job like a budget before beginning a job. Let us say that you just design a web site and the customer is angry since there are not any pictures when it is all done and said. Which might not be something you normally do, but the customer is angry because they supposed there could be graphics. This ought to have been discussed before this introduction of the undertaking.

Get It in Writing

One Of the most effective methods to make sure both parties are on precisely the exact same page is using a contract. Does this help prevent some mistakes, additionally, it protects you if a customer pulls from a job or won't pay you.

The Contract should at least contain the following:

- Names of the two parties - the freelancer and the customer
- Title endeavor
- Beginning date of job
- The job's deadline
- Milestones
- Payment conditions - if and how you are going to get payment
- certain terms or job
- Signature from the parties

The Contract should also have exemptions such as fees. This means making certain you get paid for your job even when the plug is pulled on the job. You might also need to go over copyright choices. By way of instance, you maintain ownership until the last payment is received.

Believe About all of the times that you have had an issue in your professional or personal life. I wager you'll see a frequent theme - the origin of the issue comes back to a lack of a communicating. While it might appear a little like overkill, there is nothing wrong in asking your customer for direction or feedback, keeping them updated about the status of the job through testimonials, and also simply dropping them a quick email to see how everything is moving.

Communication Not only averts any headaches, it is also an effective means to strengthen the association between you and your customer.

Be Adaptive, But Not Too Much

To Endure being a freelancer you've got to be adaptable. After allof the deadlines and also the reach of the job can change during the course of a job. But, that does not mean you need to be a pushover. Be up front with a customer and describe to them what could be achieved and as soon as it can be achieved. If that is likely to be another price, then you want to alert the customer that there'll be another fee. Thus, if you are that web designer you may add those pictures, but it is likely to cost the customer a little more income.

Tools Which Make Life Easier

Thank you To technologies, there are lots of programs and applications which could enable you to manage and communicate with customers. Some of those instruments include:

Google Apps - Not only email, you are able to share docs with customers and communicate Through discussion or Hangouts.

Nimble - Integrates all you contact, Social Networking, client Mails, and calendar.

Contactually - Manages your Customers, and gives you advice on how to Connect together.

Falcon - Integrates with 14 distinct Social Networking platforms so You are able to find out more about your clientele.

MailChimp - Lets You send bulk mails to customers to maintain them informed.

Skype - Speak or talk to your customers anywhere in the world for free.

You May also do some homework and ask your system whenever they've coped with this particular customer previously or even hunting online and seeing whether there are any complaints on places like the Better Business Bureau.

PROJECT MANAGEMENT

Since You are creating your own program, you have to get coordinated when planning out jobs. The very last thing you need is taking off to the shore for the day and realizing that you've got deadline due daily! In addition to keeping you motivated, handling jobs will be able to assist you in maintaining customers and subcontractors from the loop.

One Of the best places to begin is with a calendar which has significant deadlines or meeting dates with customers. Google Calendar, such as is a set up place to get started. There is also the amazing Sunrise Calendar which you may use on either your mobile device or desktop computer. Project Management

But, You will find powerful project management tools such as Basecamp, LiquidPlanner, Projecturf, Wrike, and Project Bubble which could keep you on course with a job. You also need to check to to-do-lists programs like Evernote, Wunderlist, Any.do, and Todoist to maintain your own life and work as a way.

Even though You have to control your projects, do not forget to spend time for boosting your new, touching base with customers, and managing tasks such as charging.

HOW TO GET PAID

Obtaining Compensated is just another one of the necessary evils that freelancers need to confront. Without getting a payment to your job, you are pretty much defeating the purpose of being in business on your own. Happily, getting paid is not as much as a hassle because it was due to applications from websites like Due.com which permit you to bill clients in only a matter of moments - and because you signed this contract. Nonetheless, you might even ensure becoming compensated by taking the next guidance.

Be A expert

If You are rude to your customers, always late on jobs, deliver subpar work, and possess an outdated site, then why would a customer make paying your bill a priority?

Consistently Be an expert by having a site which highlights your job, over delivering a job, meeting deadlines, and being respectful.

Be Adaptive With Rates and Payment Alternatives

Perhaps not All customers will have the ability to manage your prices or perhaps use all the services offered. Does that imply that you decrease their small business? Let us say that you are a marketing agency and a regional deli just would like you to help upgrade their site and put some cash into Facebook advertisements, but are not worried with you sending out media releases or composing daily articles for them. Then it is reasonable that you have prices for your customers that are only searching for a portion of their services, let us say $500 a month, as you aren't providing the entire package. Which is generally $1,500.

Additionally, You would like to take a number of types of payments from the customers. Does this make it much easier for them to cover, in addition, it accelerate the payment procedure. Most invoicing software provides you the capacity to accept eChecks, credit/debit cards, or via a payment gateway such as PayPal.

Bill Up Front

Most Lawyers need some kind of payment up front. This amount will differ from industry-to-industry, however a deposit that's 25%-50% of this quote is really common practice. Your contract must also detail if you're getting interim payments - let us say 50 percent up front, 25 percent at the center, and the last 25 percent when finished.

Invoice Immediately and Often

When You do not have recurring customers, be certain you bill weekly or immediately after the conclusion of a project. This not only keeps the money flowing into your bank accounts, in addition, it helps to ensure that you won't forget to send out this bill.

Invoicing Applications from Due.com or Invoice Ninja makes it possible for you to set-up recurring customer profiles or automatic billing. This usually means you could make an invoice in a snap or setup recurring billing, meaning that the customer's credit card or bank account is automatically deducted every month at the quantity which you're owed.

Never Work Until You Are Paid

Why Keep working on a job at no cost when you might be working for a customer which really pays for your services? As any freelancer will inform you, you can't work on another job until you are paid for the previous occupation. But that does not mean that you send an invoice and await a payment. If the date is quickly approaching, get in touch with the customer and discover what is happening. Perhaps they inadvertently lost your invoice or maybe they are out of the town.

What If a Client Does Not' Pay?

What Occurs every time a customer has not paid a bill for a outsourcing job? There are two or three different avenues which you may research.

As Previously mentioned, you may just contact the customer and ask on the status about the payment. If an email does not get an answer, you might choose to provide the customer a call or stop by their office if they're in precisely the exact same place as possible. If you are not assertive enough, possibly ask a friend, family member, colleague, or helper that has an opportunity to get hold of the customer.

If The customer will not respond to your calls or mails, after a couple of reminders, and then you might have no other choice than to look at handing the bill on to a collection agency.

CHAPTER FOUR: GIG WORKER

Non-traditional or gig Work is made of income-earning activities out traditional, long-term employer-employee relationships. We all know what it isn't. However, what is gig job? What forms of work does this contain? Before diving into amounts, it's crucial to take into account different methods for defining this particular workforce.

Approaches to defining gig work

Some definitions are Depending on the work arrangement: the relationship or contract between employees and the person or business who pays them. Conventional employees have a long-term employer-employee connection where the employee is covered by the hour annually, making a commission or salary. Outside of the arrangement, work will be momentary or project-based; employees are hired to complete a specific job or for a particular length of time. Sometimes, they've got an employer, however, the firm that pays them is different than the one where they operate. These kinds of structures are often referred to as alternate or nonstandard work arrangements, and might incorporate freelancing, temp service function, self-employment, and subcontracted work.

Other definitions of Unconventional or gig work centre on the taxation status or lawful classification of employees: the gap between employees and independent contractors. Employees get W-2 types in their companies, that are obligated to supply them certain advantages, to withhold payroll taxes, and therefore are covered by minimum wage and anti-discrimination legislation. Oftentimes, temp-agency and subcontracted work is W-2 work, but the W-2 is issued with the contracting firm in place of the firm at which the employee reports to do the job. Independent contractors, in contrast, get 1099 forms when they perform services for a business with no direct employee. Payroll taxes aren't deducted, and neither party is insured by exactly the very same regulations and rules that are applicable to conventional employees.

Finally, some Definitions derive from the character of work: about what people really do on a Daily basis. These definitions seem at certain features of work, Such as monitoring, flexibility, or lack of immediate supervision. Given that the Diversity of unconventional work, these attributes might be observed as positive or negative.

These Distinct Approaches to defining unconventional and gig work . Those working in different arrangements tend to be categorized as independent contractors with 1099 tax status, and frequently have inconsistent schedules—but maybe not necessarily. Thus, different definitions lead to different estimates of this gig workforce. Surveys most commonly inquire about labour agreements, but every definition provides significant insights to the gig market, and findings from three are introduced at the Information Hub.

Just how many gig employees are there?

There Are Lots of ways To gauge the size of this gig market and unconventional workforce. Some count the entire number of employees who take part in any sort of unconventional work. Some just count people who rely upon this work due to their main earnings. Other people rely only specific kinds of structures, such as online platform function or subcontracted arrangements. For every one of these steps, numbers vary dependent on the precise wording of questions. A closer evaluation of these similarities and differences of these definitions used in each study is found in the Research section of this Information Hub.

Over a quarter of Employees take part in the gig market in some capacity.

A few steps of this Gig market comprise any employee who participates in unconventional work in almost any capacity—offline or online, with routine or occasional involvement, and for main or supplemental earnings. Including employees who hold conventional fulltime work along with gigs, in addition to people who just conduct gig work.

MBO Partners, the Freelancers' Union, also McKinsey Global Institute3each have ran online polls of the federal workforce which signify between 25 and 30 percent of employees had participated in unconventional or gig job on a secondary or main basis from the previous month. Since large-scale public polls, like those handled by the Bureau of Labor Statistics, usually do not inquire about work, these personal polls are a few of the best quotes we have of occasional or supplementary gig employees.

The estimates vary Depending on the definition of gig work employed, the time period considered, as well as the people which has been sampled for the poll. The most significant estimate of unconventional work accessible—40 percent of their work force—is by a Government Accountability Office evaluation of General Social Survey (GSS) data, also includes standard part-time job, which many specialists wouldn't think about a unconventional arrangement.

Over one in ten Employees rely on gig job for their main income.

Greater than half of Those who take part in gig job rely on gigs to their main income. According to the latest Contingent Worker Supplement (CWS) administered by the Bureau of Labor Statistics (BLS), 10.1 percentage of employees rely on different arrangements for their principal occupation, such as temp agency function, on-call work, contracted job, and outsourcing.

This amount remained Stable since 2005, the previous year that the CWS has been conducted. Other quotes are slightly greater. In 2015, economists Lawrence Katz and Alan Krueger replicated the CWS, also estimated 15.8 percent of employees relied upon other structures as their principal occupation, though they later revised their estimate and concluded it had been considerably nearer to the 2017 Contingent Worker Supplement figures. In 2014, on the General Social Survey, 20.4 percent of employed respondents reported that an independent agreement, utilizing a similar definition to the CWS. The discrepancy between research might be the consequence of differences in sampling and methodology, or different financial conditions in the time of their research. More consistent, comprehensive data collection is necessary to be able to understanding the association between involvement in unconventional work and wider economic problems.

Some Personal polls Ask about fulltime gig job, and produce comparable estimates of fulltime gig employees, between 10 and 13% of their workforce. Synthesizing current studies, we estimate that individuals who rely solely on gig work so as to create a living include less than half of gig employees. The remainder of those who choose gigs do this on a supplemental basis, along with a part - or fulltime conventional work or another income source. Additional study is required to completely comprehend how pre school work fits into the wider labor market and the way it contributes to family incomes.

Approximately one percent of Workers frequently use online platforms to contact work opportunities.

Online platforms such as Uber, Lyft, and TaskRabbit garner much press attention. These programs, which connect employees with particular kinds of gigs, just represent a small section of unconventional workers. Whether measured using polls, tax returns, or bank account action, approximately 1 percent of employees have employed online platforms to organize work from the last month. Some estimates are higher since they use a wide description of internet work, also include selling products or accepting online surveys, besides performing services organized online, or inquire about involvement over a longer time period.

Gig work necessitates new Ways of quantifying work

Many Kinds of gig work Don't fit neatly into the classes we generally use to assess the workforce. Concepts like"job" and"company" do not necessarily make sense, meaning that we may need new methods of asking questions so as to accurately quantify workers that are unconventional. Some investigators have taken new strategies. By way of instance, the Federal Reserve inquires about income-earning actions instead of tasks, since people might not describe everyday sources of income since jobs. In another fresh strategy, the Internet Association quantified the amount of online-platform accounts held by employees, reporting 23.9 million balances.

All them Procedures is discussed more completely from the Data Hub's Research department, together with information about the sampling and processes of every questionnaire. Despite several gaps, across these steps, unconventional workers are a substantial portion of the workforce.

Who participates in The gig market?

Who are gig market Employees?

Gig and Non-traditional employees are people, old and young, reside across the nation, and reflect the racial, cultural, and socioeconomic diversity of the nation. Even though there are a few patterns in the demographic makeup of the population, in addition, there are a great deal of discrepancies between polls. A lot of the inconsistency stems from differences in the way each questionnaire defines nontraditional work, since distinct groups are disproportionately represented in various sorts of arrangements.

There's not a single, Normal gig employee

Age

Overall, individuals who Take part in unconventional work are somewhat more likely to be younger than conventional employees. Assessing different work structures, freelancers are usually elderly, whereas temp-agency employees and online-platform employees are usually younger.

Gender

Breakdowns of this gig Workforce by sex change by survey; a few report there are far more men than women, along with many others that there are far more women than men. This inconsistency comes from the fact that women and men take part in various kinds of unconventional work and in various ways. Men are more likely than girls to take part in online labor platforms, and also to rely on unconventional work fulltime. Girls, on the other hand, are more likely to make supplemental income and also to work part-time compared to guys, fitting patterns of employment generally. Women are also especially likely to take part in multi or direct advertising and also to sell products online.

Hurry

In conclusion, the Racial makeup of this unconventional work force is very similar to that of their general workforce. Just like sex, however, analyzing the various forms of unconventional work informs a more nuanced narrative. Agency temps, on-call, and contract business workers are more likely to be African American or Hispanic, whereas Managers, consultants, and independent contractors are more likely to be whitened. People of colour, then, are more inclined to maintain unconventional arrangements which are reduced and provide less flexibility to employees.

Education degrees

On most polls, the Unconventional workforce as a whole is slightly more educated than the total workforce. On the other hand, the educational attainment changes by special arrangement. Freelancers are somewhat more likely than traditional employees to have a postgraduate level. Conversely, temp-agency and on-call employees are less likely to have a high school degree.

Geography

Non-traditional Employees are more prone than traditional employees to reside within a metropolitan place. There's a greater concentration of those workers in Western nations, using a particularly large part from the San Francisco Bay Area, in which lots of online platform firms got their start.

We have few data on Just how much gig work really pays.

Lots of the concepts We use to measure and consider earnings don't apply to unconventional arrangements. By definition, many gigs have been covered by the job or job, meaning that the concept of an hourly salary doesn't necessarily apply. Additionally, many unconventional employees are responsible for deducting expenses, earning their gross profits to W-2 salaries, where living wage calculations are established.

Since individuals turn to Unconventional work for vastly different reasons, their fiscal requirements and expectations likewise disagree. It is difficult to understand if low monthly earnings will be caused by low pay and bad work requirements, or the options of employees who might not count on gig income to satisfy basic requirements. What's more, some kinds of unconventional work supply low salary and lead to financial uncertainty, but some deliver much-needed earnings to smooth volatility out of low-quality traditional occupations.

Regardless of the challenges Of measuring gig-work earnings, we have some advice about how earnings differ between unconventional arrangements. Freelancers' earning are very similar to above conventional employees, whereas temp-agency and on-call employees generally have lower earnings. Additionally, people working independently to supplement a different source of earnings tend to create greater than people who rely solely on work.

The independent Work force is heterogeneous

Taken together, these Demographic data imply that the unconventional work force is profoundly segmented. Some work pays especially well, provides high levels of versatility and management, and will be kept by advantaged classes, frequently on a supplemental basis. Other unconventional work offers low salary, and will be held by disadvantaged groups, that frequently rely upon it for their principal livelihood.

The gig work force is Not a single homogeneous group. Assessing the differences of experiences and needs in this population is equally as critical as understanding its importance concerning conventional employees.

What kinds of work are Performed through gigs?

Non-traditional work Exists across a broad variety of jobs. It might consist of designing sites, forcing, management consulting, maintenance work, and much more. Because unconventional work is generally characterized by how it's structured instead of the material of this job, it blurs traditional boundaries. Divisions such as blue collar versus white collar, manual versus intellectual labour, or support versus products do not necessarily apply. Work in each these classes can be a part of this gig market, based on how it's organized.

Building and Services take the direct

Gig work could—and Does—occur in just about any business, from petroleum extraction to health care. Across polls, the building sector has the maximum proportion of unconventional work agreements: nearly a quarter of construction employees are in different work arrangements. Gig work in the building business, however, isn't brand new. Carpenters, contractors,

contractors, and technicians have tended to operate independently for a long time. Professional and business services, a diverse group which includes architects, accountants, janitors, and administrative support employees, have likewise had a high nevertheless comparatively steady speed of independent structures.

Rates of growth change across industries

Other businesses have Experienced growth in the last ten years. The transport industry has witnessed an increase in the amount of workers in different arrangements, and notably independent contracting in the previous twenty decades. Although more information is required to understand , rideshare drivers, such as those for Uber and Lyft, might be supporting this leap.

Additionally, a few Kinds of gig work don't fit into traditional industry classifications, like the selling of home made products on the web.

What are the Experiences of gig employees?

Just as there is not 1 typical gig employee or one typical occupation, there's not 1 approach to describe the experience of engaging in the gig market. Lack of adventures is a fundamental motif of unconventional work.

Most gig employees Report being fulfilled by their work agreements

Across polls, more Than two thirds of unconventional employees report being satisfied with their job agreements. Many report enjoying the management this work permits them within their period along with also the flexibility of scheduling. Additionally, many origin their pride from the income their position work supplies. Oftentimes, gig job income smooths shaky earnings from a conventional occupation. In others, individuals turn to gig job to manage financial desperation, or just to meet basic requirements and cover the bills. Other people utilize their own gig earnings for travel or other discretionary expenditures. Another desirable facet can be these structures' low barrier to entry. Some sorts of unconventional work are available for employees who might otherwise struggle to go into the labor market, such as immigrant and previously incarcerated populations.

When requested, survey Respondents have a tendency to state they pursue unconventional workout of choice instead of from necessity. Studying levels of satisfaction and perceived benefits and challenges, however, gives greater insight to the adventures of the work than inquiring about motives, because folks will probably explain their own plight as the consequence of decision regardless of financial or other pressures which affect them.

Financial volatility And accessibility to benefits are important challenges

Although a Lot of gig Employees find gratification, they also face real challenges. Most conspicuous is the absence of consistent, predictable earnings, reported as a significant concern among gig employees across surveys. The problem in predicting earnings contributes to both economic and mental stress; gig employees report higher rates of stress compared to conventional employees.

Another challenge Confronted by unconventional workers is that their lack of access to benefits, such as health insurance and retirement programs. Employees in different arrangements are somewhat less likely than conventional workers to get medical insurance from their own employer, and to get health insurance in any way. On the latest BLS Contingent Worker Supplement, 84 percent of standard workers had health care policy, with over half getting insurance from their own employer. One of temp-agency employees, just 67 percent had coverage, and just 12 percent obtained insurance from a company. One of independent builders, 75 percent had policy, most of whom needed to get this insurance by themselves.

The Majority of those that are Left uninsured by job find policy throughout the Affordable Care Act market, meaning that this market is very valuable among this people—unconventional employees are over three times more prone than conventional workers to depend on the market, and internet platform employees are nearly four times more likely. Despite improved access to health care throughout ACA, as many as a quarter of unconventional workers report forgoing medical therapy due to high expenses.

Even fewer can Accessibility retirement programs. Just 7% of temp-agency employees, 30 percent of workers employees, and 38 percent of contract-company employees can get low-income compared with 46 percent of conventional workers. Concerns over gains are pressing for employees who rely on gig job because of their principal earnings, since side-by-side employees may still access advantages through a conventional occupation.

Non-traditional Employees aren't alone, however, in their own concerns about work-related advantages. Conventional employees also report this being a significant subject of concern. Within the last thirty decades, the supply of employer-sponsored retirement and health insurance has decreased over companies, particularly those in the service industry. Even though the challenge of procuring advantages is especially acute for gig employees, it isn't unique for them.

The adventures of gig Employees are polarized

Benefits and Challenges of gig work aren't evenly dispersed. Function that a few turn to so as to smooth out or supplement their earnings is the origin of high monetary volatility to many others. What brings freedom and flexibility for some attracts instability and insecurity for many others. The adventures of unconventional employees are polarized, demonstrating real challenges to a employees while offering opportunities to other people. These gaps in expertise are inextricable in how we consider the gig market. The requirements of a supplemental high-skill freelancer are all basically different than the requirements of a full-time subcontracted worker, and addressing the challenges faced by gig employees means paying attention to the diversity of expertise. Researchers will need to further explore the distinction of encounters of non-traditional workers to be able to better comprehend the variety of needs of the population.

What's the future of gig work?

The Character of work Structures is in regular. Though we lack large scale, consistent statistics on unconventional work structures, over the previous two decades, the amount of individuals engaged in gig work in some capacity has improved across most steps.

Continued Technological advancement retains the capability to ease additional gains in gig work involvement. Online platform technology has produced new types of work potential, and as this and associated technologies grow, they will likely continue to form the work force and bring about modifications to the gig market.

Maybe most Significantly, the dawn of gig work isn't an isolated trend, but one associated with wide shifts in the market. Globalization and technological improvements put pressure on organizations to respond quickly to market fluctuations. Preventing labour through unconventional arrangements eases these rapid answers, allowing companies to swiftly accommodate the size of the workforce. Some have noticed that this will allow organizations to boost their short-term profits. Seen in this light, unconventional and gig work is a basic part of today's market, therefore is not likely to dissipate soon.

Yet, there are Also reasons to be careful in making predictions. If recent changes have informed us with certainty, it is that calling the future is risky business. The newly published Contingent Worker Supplement demonstrates that the amount of individuals relying on other work arrangements for their principal job has stayed steady over the previous twenty decades. Gig work, particularly online platform function, has large turnover. By several measures, rates of expansion in stage work have begun to slow, possibly approaching a point of saturation where there are fewer new entrants. Actually, current growth rates are unsustainable; when the observed expansion of Uber drivers continued prevailed, each American employee are an Uber motorist in five decades.

We want new and better Data to consider the future of work

The unconventional Workforce is fundamental to the current market. Irrespective of discrepancies between predictions and measures for the near future, the gig market signifies a fundamental shift in the manner in which work has been performed and the connection between employees and businesses. Employees are being asked to accept responsibility for their economic security, as firms try to respond quickly to market pressures and conditions.

The main Tool that we will need to better predict future trends in gig work will be continued and expanded data collection and investigation. As work arrangements vary, theories we rely on—occupations, companies, salary—will take on new significance. As the labour market and the world change, we want ongoing, thoughtful information collection and evaluation to better understand the current employees and their demands.

CHAPTER FIVE:
EVOLUTION OF GIG ECONOMY

The future of work is Obscured by two contrasting visions. One is a daydream using a notebook and a sea view, where highly-skilled function is divorced from any specific site. Another is a nightmare of drudgery, where hours have been spent plodding the corridors of a giant warehouse pushing a trolley using a robotic earpiece telling us to walk farther and faster. Both dreams take their cue from the excitable narratives swirling round the "gig market" a concept where there is not any easy, commonly agreed definition.

To some it means white Collar piecework, to the others the west of unregulated electronic sweatshops. The Undercover Economist, Tim Harford, describes it as "small amounts for miniature jobs" that does not feel sufficient while some are describing a related job marketplace whose worth could soon run into thousands of bucks.

The Individual Cloud

Gigging itself has its own Origins from the 1920s jazz scene but its present revival is more electronic than musical. Mckinsey, so frequently the origin of excitable small business speech, provides the most sober expression, calling it "contingent work that's transacted on an electronic market."

For the boosters, the Gig market is the start of "the individual cloud" where companies are going to have the ability to overcome skills shortages and liberate themselves in the boundaries of location. The loudest of those voices are coming out of the platforms where this market has been assembled, such as MBAandCompany, whose CEO Daniel Callaghan lately informed the Financial Times: "You are now able to get exactly what you want, whenever you need, exactly the way you would like it," he states. "And since they are not workers you do not need to take care of labour regulations and hassles."

The evolution Economist, Guy Standing, sees something entirely different. He's coined the expression "precariat" (an unhappy union of this precarious and proletariat) to explain a new and expanding underclass. When most economists have whined about jobless expansion because the last financial catastrophe, Reputation looks to the future and sees"growth-less occupations" because the true matter. He foresees the spread of low productivity projects with cellar salaries and virtually no advantages like health insurance or pensions.

In Summary, the gig Market is an idea that will reflect the prejudices of its audience. A fast look in its emerging hierarchy provides some perspective.

The strongest thing You're able to say about the gig market is the fact that it is smaller than the hype surrounding it. The prominence of businesses such as Uber, whose fleet of motorists aren't workers, and also the giant electronic yard sale that's Etsy, where people are able to flip handicraft hobbies to some negative income, has captured the public imagination. The gig market has featured in america election cycle together with Democrats attacking it in the left and Republicans lauding it in the right.

Showing up anyplace But the information

However, a thorough evaluation of government information shows small has Changed in the past ten years, with the proportion of Americans announcing themselves self-employed declining. Some 6.5 percentage of America's 157-million-strong workforce were employed in 2015, down from a high of almost 9 percent from the 1990s. The percentage of employees with multiple jobs is just as stagnant.

Across the pond in Britain, freelancers make up only 2 percent of their work force, a figure that's mostly unchanged from the previous 15 years. It is possible that the gain in the amount of Britons declaring themselves self-evident might comprise some gigsters but it might also be explained by more conventional kinds of self-employment. The three growth areas in UK self control are hairdressing, cleaning and management consultancy. Yes, it is possible that a few of those advisers are investing in their solutions around HourlyNerd or among its rivals but these businesses were growing before anybody mentioned"gig". Conversely amounts of self-employed cab drivers are in decline. Since Lawrence Mishel, president of the Economic Policy Institute puts it"proof of an exploding gig market is showing up anywhere but the information."

When it did appear in The information it was a false alert. Most sensible analysts are agreed when the wonks in the US Governmental Accountability Office declared in 2015 the proportion of contingent workers had jumped from 30.6 percent in 2006 to 40.4 percent, it did not mean much. Their approaches were debatable and their definition of determined work was so extensive it comprised everyone not in fulltime traditional jobs.

The revolution will Not be announced

The obvious idea is That official statistics are a lousy place to go looking. Not everybody declares gig earnings, particularly if the job is completed along with a conventional occupation. A lot of don't think about leasing out their seat or their automobile for a kind of paid work, therefore that they do not tell census employees about it, let alone the tax collector.

A fairer premise is The gig market is at its infancy and its expansion will not be linear. The large beast of the emerging market, Upwork, is cited as proof of this: that the individual cloud system required 10 years to reach $1bn earnings but hopes to increase those ten-fold at the subsequent six decades.

To rebut the skeptics, Economists such as Harvard's Larry Katz have escalated into'1099' filings such as signs. When a company, non-profit or government service pays a person greater than $600 annually in non-employee rcimbursement that is the kind they file with the Internal Revenue Service (IRS). These figures are on the upswing. A deep dive into government data finds that non-employer companies (sole proprietors) are up from 12% of the US workforce in the close of the 1990s to 16 percent in 2013 (no information as). It has prompted some observers to assert that we've got a"1099 market".

Daniel Tomlinson, by the Resolution Foundation at London, States that:"quantifying the gig market is not simple and authorities would be wise to follow the case of the US Department of Labor who've declared they will shortly be collecting data regarding the status of contingent employees"

But he warns Against overstating the fluctuations in the labour market and the magnitude of contingent functioning:"This is not to say the gig market will remain small; adoption of new technologies by existing companies, disruption by new innovative companies and the National Living Wage are likely to contribute to the rise of the gig market in the years ahead"

21st Century legislation

Therefore the rise of the gig Market is real, it is simply not as big or as quickly as some have indicated. However, it will pose very real challenges to company and policymakers. We are seeing the most evident manifestation of this is that the legal struggles being waged against Uber. Are their drivers workers or not? The business says not but a number of the drivers take the opposing perspective.

This is where the job Of Alan Krueger, previously an economic advisor to President Barack Obama and Seth Harris in Cornell University come in.

"There's now Much doubt regarding if your Uber motorist—or Lyft motorist, or TaskRabbit useful person, or Thumbtack private trainer—will probably be judged a worker or independent contractor from the legal system," writes Harris.

The Krueger-Harris response would be to make another group of Employee from the grey area between"employee" and"independent contractor" known as"independent employee". Their proposal would enable gig employees to join or form a union but it would not induce them to compensated vacation or defense against being fired. It might allow companies like Lyft to provide medical insurance or pensions because benefits without the stress that the courts could tag them companies.

The cynics will Rightly wonder just how a lot of the sharing market behemoths would really wish to supply advantages unless legally obliged to do so. Meanwhile, the very first job advertisements have started to look for C-level Chief Freelance Relationship Officers. A current Randstad gift report discovered that almost half of HR leaders were considering how to reply to the gig market.

HR specialist Mervyn Dinnen Claims that freelance dating officer Is"a part whose time has come" and devoting more focus being paid to how businesses handle their standing among freelancers. The Freelancers Union and their #FreelanceIsn'tFree effort have shown how gig employees can make themselves noticed and gain grip. Our universe of work has been reshaped but its final form is going to be contested.

The Way to hire freelancers

If you want Help using a short term job, employing a freelancer might be a fantastic selection. You are able to spend less on job benefits and taxes related to part-time and full workers, and have access to the type of experience you want. Companies generally hire freelance programmers, developers, designers and authors.

Here is our guide on The way to hire a freelancer and a couple of suggestions about the best way best to make this agreement work for both parties:

Hire Managers online:

When looking for those Professionals on the internet, you've got ample choices. Think about utilizing:

Freelancing platforms. While the gig market might not be a booming fashion , you are still able to find many fantastic writing, layout along with other creative salespeople on the internet. Committed platforms allow you to research salespeople' profiles and place your own projects. Additionally they have rating systems that will assist you evaluate professionals according to testimonials from past gigs.

Freelancing Platforms

Upwork

Freelancer

Fiverr

Guru

Hubstaff Present

Portfolio websites . Portfolio sites offer a peek into people's work. These websites are particularly useful once you want to find creative professionals (e.g. freelancer designers, copywriters and programmers). Post a project, research profiles and reach out to people interested in freelancing. You might also utilize Boolean search on Google to find profiles that fit your criteria.

Portfolio websites

Behance

Dribbble

Carbonmade

Stack Overflow

GitHub

Social platforms. Aside from the typical suspects, such as Twitter and Facebook, additional programs may be useful also. By way of instance, on Reddit, you may use a subreddit to describe your job or locate subreddits of individuals offering their solutions. Additionally, you may search websites such as Meetup to find groups made for freelancers.

Social Media

Twitter/ Facebook

Reddit

Meetup

LinkedIn

You could also Directly place a project for salespeople on project boards or advertising websites, such as Craigslist and Really .

Evaluate Freelancer candidates

Quality of work is that the Most significant criterion. To appraise a freelancer:

Read testimonials . If you're utilizing a freelancing system, then start looking to some freelancer's testimonials from customers. Figure out if any problems have come up. Should they have consistently lower ratings, consider different freelancers.

Study their portfolio. Investigate the projects they've worked before. If you're trying to find some degree of experience or particular abilities, select freelancers who've worked on jobs like yours.

Provide a smaller paid job . Request them to function on part of this bigger project you are hiring , or an independent endeavor. Judge the quality of the job firsthand. Pilot missions are particularly useful once you're hiring freelancers to get large projects or thinking about placing them on retainer.

Meet them. A face-to-face freelancers might not always be possible, but attempt to arrange an internet meeting through telephone or movie . Speak to them, describe your job in detail and allow them to ask questions. The top freelancers will be careful to understand your needs and will indicate what they have to complete the undertaking.

The best way to handle freelancers

Contract employees who Were hired to compose a blog article or designing a symbol might be simple to control. However if you hire freelancers to aid with larger-scale jobs, you might have to place a little excess thought into how to handle them correctly.

Here are 3 hints For managing Managers:

Communicate thoroughly

To convey your Expectations efficiently, supply:

- Deadlines. As you might not be the freelancer's just customer, talk and establish deadlines so that you may get your work in time.
- Milestones. Break big jobs into landmarks—manageable segments for

which freelancers receive some of their entire payment. Milestones help you monitor progress and assist your salespeople feel more protected. And, paying output sets the focus on quality instead of the amount of hours spent on the job.

- Vision. If you'd like a freelancer to redesign your site, make them understand how you envision it. Communicate your needs upfront, as well as clearly as you can, to be certain you're both on precisely the exact same page.
- Context. Describe how this job or sub-project fits into a bigger project or plan. A fantastic freelancer will figure out ways to tailor their output to align with your overall company plan.

Classify freelancers Properly

Freelancers are Different from the workers because they are not bound to a particular company. This usually means they don't obtain the benefits that a worker does, but they also get to perform in their own provisions with very little supervision.

When handling Freelancers, it is important to maintain this type of structure intact. Businesses frequently misclassify their employees as independent contractors, but their job requirements indicate they are in fact employees. The U.S. Internal Revenue Service (IRS) penalizes instances of misclassifications and consequently, some companies must pay hefty fines, in addition to back taxes and wages.

The way you treat Managers as a complete things, as well as the standards That courts use change . Butgenerally, it is best to not:

- Dictate programs . Specifying an outcome and deadlines is vital, but telling your salespeople just the number of hours to work or through which time period may encourage legal trouble.
- Assign crucial tasks. A freelancer's job shouldn't be an essential component of your manufacturing procedures or the support your company provides.
- Cover their prices . Independent contractors or contractors create

their own investments at a job and shoulder some risk of loss. Avoid paying for tools, equipment, training, transport or other expenses.

- Supervise their job . You could sometimes check in with your freelancer to obtain an upgrade on a job (whether offsite or onsite). However, it's ideal to refrain from requesting them to follow particular work techniques or report regularly for you personally.
- Utilize a salary-like payment arrangement . Freelancers have different payment arrangements than workers. You can either pay by the hour or by outputsignal. Obtaining a level amount occasionally may turn your salespeople right in to workers, in the opinion of law.
- Be their sole customer. Firms have very little control over this, however a freelancer shouldn't be economically determined by you. Make sure you do not provide your freelancer so much work they're not able to receive different customers.
- Hire freelancers only If you want a particular job or job done. If you realize that you require a person on a daily basis, or you feel that the need to supply certain instructions, employ a part-time or fulltime worker rather.

Show your admiration

If you are Happy Using a freelancer's job, make motions to keep them on your radar. Later on, you might have to employ them for a job or perhaps provide them employment. Here are a couple of things that you may do:

- Leave favorable testimonials in their profiles.
- Thank them openly through a societal networking account.
- Direct them to a spouse or connected company as freelancers.
- Invite them to observe the conclusion of a job they had been a part of.
- All these activities Help establish your respect to your job your salespeople do for you, and will only boost your company brand.

Freelancers bring Experience and expertise when you want them. Should you choose some time to employ and handle staffs correctly, you may reap the benefits of a mutually beneficial cooperation.

As a freelancer, and instead of an Employee, you need to locate duties (rather than a project) to earn a living from your company. This usually means heading out to seek customers.

Assignment: that Means a contract which the freelancer negotiates with every customer. The missions could be short or long, spaced out or shut together. They are frequently unpredictable (with respect to their length, frequency and value) and that could create problems if you would like to make income.

To protect yourself in the face of the unpredictability Of missions, it is important that you understand how to locate fresh prospects on demand (i.e. if the need presents itself) and keep tabs on these at a prospection document (also referred to as a marketing file or customer file).

Fortunately There Are Lots of sources of chance for Independent employees, which we will explore in this program, over these chapters:

1. The platforms, sites, programs and marketplaces that present salespeople to customers.

2. The bureaus along with other service industry intermediaries, that frequently recruit employees to perform services;

3. The little ads sites and employment sites using search filters for salespeople;

4. Immediate prospection for customers.

Then, together, we'll compose the primary document of your Marketing approach: the freelancer marketing action plan, which brings along the chances to pursue in accordance with your profile.

The different Kinds of stage

The United Kingdom had over 6,000,000 independent employees in 2016 as well as on the work market, the tendency is for the growth of the gig market (job in the kind of duties for salespeople). In the face of these improvements, a lot of platforms have emerged to attract gig employees and prospective customers together.

There Are Lots of Kinds of site and program that Provide to present independent employees and customers:

• Platforms: authentic freelancer"programs" handle the connection with the customer from begin to finish (quote, invoicing, price setting, project management, quality management and customer service) and externalise service supply to franchisees. The programs give the online tools to ease the job of the gig employees (e.g. Uber's GPS, or even TextMaster's internet translation port). In the event the service is performed on the internet, the freelancer doesn't have any interaction with the end customer. These programs remunerate themselves using a commission that range from 10% to 40 percent. Cases of programs: Uber, TextMaster, italki, Verbling, Deliveroo, UberEats, JustEat, DogBuddy, Pawshake, Quiqup

• Marketplaces (leading to solutions): marketplaces are all websites which mention the vendors—the salespeople—and also have a method for making contact, so that customers can dictate their solutions. All these marketplaces render more flexibility into the gig employees concerning services provided and their costs, and they do not intervene in the cooperation. But, marketplaces secure payment and supply high visibility. In exchange, they bill commissions of 5% to 20 percent. The customers are usually professionals (companies). Cases of marketplaces: Fiverr, Malt, Task Rabbit, Upwork, GIG, Guru

• Job search sites : overall online job boards, and while lots of the jobs posted are for job, you will also find freelance and short-term gigs. Examples of occupation websites: Truly , Dragon , Reed, StudentJob, E4S, Gumtree, UK Classifieds

• Professional directories or institutions , such as: The Organization of Independent Professionals and the Self-Employed, The UK Copywriters Directory, ProZ (for language professionals)

For The interest of simplicity, in this class we will use the expression"platforms" to imply these options.

To operate successfully with a stage, several variables Have to be taken into consideration.

· You Have to Pick the most suitable platforms to your profile along with your company proposal so as to Prevent disappointment and to concentrate your campaign;

· Then, You Have to subscribe to some of programs to Receive Normal missions;

· Last, you want to perfect your own profile to draw interest on sites, in which the competition can be fierce.

Select the programs that best suit your profile

Platforms Provide many chances for independent employees, in most Areas and for many budgets.

Return to your company proposal and listen to each of the Following points:

· The Reach of your homework (what interests you);

· Your functioning conditions (if not you will traveling, the hours you are available);

· Your minimum hourly fee.

Then create a list of those programs that match you and navigate them, Assessing their service provides correspond nicely with your different criteria, and if they are acceptable for you.

Maintain An open mind concerning the goals of these programs, which may not correspond precisely with what you would like, but may bring you additional benefits you haven't wondered about. To understand that, look at occupations offered on these websites, or ask other men and women using these (e.g. through social networks).

Now it is your turn! Use an internet search engine to research the Platforms linked to your line of business. Hunt:"freelance platform" + your function (e.g."freelance consultant platform") to locate assignments that match you. Or begin with the illustrations given above.

Professional Directories and local/national/international institutions for the profession or line of business may be handy for discovering missions. They do not work like platforms. A number of them require registration. They occasionally introduce customers and salespeople and may have the benefit of high visibility. As an instance, that is true for ProZ.com, which will be a directory that has turned into a true benchmark website for discovering freelance translators. Do not neglect this course.

Utilize the Identical research method as possible for programs, simply Placing in"Professional association" or"Professional directory" followed by your livelihood or service provide.

Take several subscriptions out, for flexible and routine assignments

You will realize that there's a vast array of platforms. It is Enough to navigate them to understand if the soul of the service fulfills your fantasies or your organization proposition. .

The Benefit of those platforms is that their visibility, Which brings large numbers of customers, and which will often allow you to function to purchase. A number of them are used so much that it is sufficient to link to them to discover missions.

As an account because of this, the prices are somewhat less Than you can negotiate directly with customers. But as soon as you're listed on these programs, you are going to save yourself the expenses of canvassing for organization, project management, invoicing and customer support. In addition they guarantee repayment, which reduces the non-payment danger that you run as a freelancer.

As Each platform differs, take care to look at their working procedures and the warranties you will receive, when you register. This information is generally on the"How does this work?" Pages or beneath the FAQ (Frequently Asked Questions) headings of these sites.

Be aware that it is not feasible to negotiate using a stage. Deadlines, scope and budgets of missions are often determined by the site or directly from the customer. It is an issue of "take it or leave it" chances.

Carefully Read the general terms and conditions, which behave as a contract and then set the principles for the customer and freelancer.

You risk nothing by registering several Platforms and by accepting only the missions which make sense for you. Generally, not being busy will not count against you.

Thus, subscribe to as many programs as you can (while optimizing Your own profiles), so as to raise your odds of becoming routine missions.

Safeguard Your company by working for many customers (and, so, for many platforms if you are just picking this course). In the event of problem with a few of your customers, you're going to have the ability to rely on other people to ensure you continuity of revenue!

Increase your Odds of success on the programs

Competition is very fierce on These sites. In reality, it's the path that is simplest to take and can be used by the vast majority of freelancers.

Here are a few Techniques to be able to draw the interest of consumers in the surface of the contest:

· Carefully prepare your profile: include a photograph to your webpage, a well drafted description of your services (or your own small business proposal adjusted to match your stage), and examples of prior work or client testimonials.

· Be responsive: platform customers are usually in a rush. On certain platforms, they are easily able to contact a number of salespeople at once and select the person who replies quickest. Ensure that you respond to them fast, so as to raise your probability of getting homework. Activate email notifications when a customer contacts you (via your profile settings on the stage). Regularly check your mails and your own messages on the programs.

· Provide high quality work: place the emphasis on quality for your homework. Take good care of your writing if corresponding with your clientele. Be cautious with service delivery and also notify the customer of any delay or trouble struck. In the end of your mission, do not be afraid to ask your customer to provide you a score, a recommendation or a review on the stage, which will boost your visibility.

Some Platforms incorporate quality in their algorithm, to provide priority to salespeople that take the most difficulty, by sending them assignments and emphasizing their profiles or perhaps by providing expert-level remuneration (e.g. Textmaster for web content authors).

· Personalise your answers : whenever you respond to an offer on a stage, compose a personalised answer for every customer. Cutting and pasting as requests come will be evident, and doing so could hazard you losing the focus and assurance of the possible customer. Do not be afraid to pick up the phrases employed by the customer to show them that you have taken account of the requirements and that you are the ideal person to fulfill them.

CHAPTER SIX:
HOW TO CAPITALIZE IT AS A COMPANY OR A FREELANCER

Here's a truth that May surprise you.

Adobe's Function in Progress Study 2016 demonstrated as many as one-third of U.S. office employees had a second occupation . And over half (56 percent) predicted we'd have multiple work later on. A LinkedIn study also forecasts that 43 percent of those U.S. Workforce is going to be included of freelancers by 2020.

This is known as the'gig Market '—an ecosystem where freelancing is your first or at least a significant source of income for tens of thousands of individuals around the globe.

For freelancers, this Means additional flexibility, added income and many other advantages. However, employers gain from the gig market also—the largest gains being cost and time efficiencies. Firms are now picking up with this trend and making way for more salespeople to combine them on board.

But before we enter The way it is possible to reevaluate it as a business or as a freelancer, let us take a peek at what the gig market is—and more folks may wind up getting"gigs" than good old routine tasks—to know this from the bottom up.

What's the Gig Economy Growing?

The gig market is Witnessing phenomenal growth as it presents several advantages for both businesses in addition to freelancers.

Benefits for Businesses

The gig market offers Compelling cost advantages and enables businesses to hire better talent. Here is how...

On-demand experience

Companies can hire On-demand experience. It is possible to seek the services of a specialist demonstration designer or an search engine optimization specialist, even in the event that you don't have the funds to employ them full time, or do not have sufficient work for them to warrant a fulltime function.

Scaling Up Quickly

Hiring on-demand Experience also enables companies to rapidly add gift whilst scaling up the group , and conversely, downsize without needing to fire full-time workers.

Access International Talent

Companies also get Access to ability from various cities and even from around the world. Hiring individuals from several places like Eastern Europe or Asia is also a significant cost saver.

Round-the-clock operate

Freelancers out of Across the globe are also useful once you want work. This is not just necessary for service groups. Additionally, it is valuable for jobs that have dependencies. Delegate a few jobs to a team from the Philippines when your day ends and they'll be done once you hit office following morning.

Produce New Business Models

The gig market makes It feasible to create completely new business models which could grow extremely quickly. Businesses like AirBnB, Uber, Deliveroo, Fiverr have been in a position to experience extraordinary growth because their service delivery staff is completely built up of salespeople. That sort of expansion would be rather impossible to replicate by constructing an in-house staff.

Save Benefits

Freelancers do not have To be compensated medical, retirement and other benefits, which can be a very attractive price saving. But a lawsuit between Uber from the united kingdom suggests that nations may enact laws in future that make it compulsory for businesses to pay rewards to particular kinds of freelancers.

Save Hiring Expenses

Employing is a costly And time-consuming procedure. In the end, companies do not need to wind up hiring someone who's not a ideal fit. This makes it essential to construct large talent acquisition groups. But, freelancers may be hired much quicker since it is not deemed to be high-risk a choice.

Benefits for Freelancers

People's expectations From existence are evolving—particularly for millennials.

More people are seeking Better work-life equilibrium and much more flexibility. We favor a lifestyle where we could handle more matters and experimentation with our professions—going the additional mile in figuring out exactly what we like to perform.

Additionally, polls From ManpowerGroup, the Freelancers Union and ReportLinker have discovered these reasons why workers prefer to freelancer:

- A stressful job environment
- Opportunities to understand and progress their livelihood
- More purposeful work
- Better pay/side revenue
- Greater esteem and empowerment
- Gig Economy Domains

Based on Katz and Krueger, more than half of this gig Market's jobs majorly come in four businesses—health care, education, structure, and professional and business services. Other noteworthy categories from the gig market include mathematical and computer, social and community services, private care, legal services, transport and warehousing, information and communications, and public management.

Listed below are a Couple of noteworthy Domains:

Software and Tech

Tech jobs will be the Highest paid at the gig market. A growing number of organizations are hiring freelance developers in domain names like profound learning, blockchain, cryptocurrency, virtual reality, robotics and so forth.

Marketing and Revenue

Marketing and sales Associated jobs are a few of the most frequent from the gig market. Including content writing, social networking promotion, SEO, security design, video editing, etc.. Revenue jobs typically involve actions around prospecting like database construction and database affirmation.

Customer Support

Customer Care is Additionally rising as a gig market section. Liveops is a business which engages freelancers in a version very similar to Uber. Actually, businesses like Home Depot or even AAA are participating freelance representatives as part of the service staff.

Instruction

Instruction is one of The largest gig market domain names. Many teachers decide to work beyond the classroom, so making extra income by teaching pupils who want additional one-on-one assistance.

Real Estate

Property requires Understanding of the marketplace. Sale and purchase choices can not be made with no careful evaluation of if the deal could be rewarding enough to yield returns. Hence, companies start looking for experienced men and women who understand the industry well to assist them with information regarding trends in the marketplace that they've been too tightly a part of. Attorneys, building managers and architects are currently joining the freelance community as advisers.

Cab Aggregators

Cab aggregators bridge That the demand-supply gap by providing drivers independence within their driving program, ensuring motorists are monetizing their strength and time.

Food Delivery

Delivery being an Essential portion of meals delivery startups, it's necessary to have additional hands-on board. Having brought it all on line with technologies, food shipping startups hire freelancer riders that make deliveries within their spare time.

How can you create the Most from this gig market?

While being a part of The gig market has its advantages, it will have its own challenges. Where there is liberty, there's responsibility—particularly without a managers to oversee how freelancers are utilizing their time.

Both companies and Freelancers will need to keep certain things in your mind to get the most from this gig market. Below are a few of the very helpful hints.

If you are an employer

You May Have worked With freelancers earlier or it might be your very first time in any situation, there are invariably a few things that would ensure things move smoothly when working together.

Ensure They are Concentrated

Based on McKinsey, there are just four Types of freelancers:

Free brokers , who knowingly choose independent work and derive their main income from it

Regular earners, who utilize separate work for supplemental earnings and do this by alternative

Reluctants, who make their main living from separate work but might prefer conventional occupations

Financially strapped, who do supplemental separate work from necessity

The 1 thing shared To all them is the simple fact that they are always juggling numerous jobs at one time, which could frequently impact their attention. Consequently, it's essential to make sure your timelines are completely clear from the start.

The Majority of the time, it is Better to work with agents that are free, only since they're completely determined by freelance work because of their earnings. They'll take your job very seriously and will provide the highest quality.

But occasionally, It is a fantastic option to go with casual individuals that want to find out—because they frequently tend to devote effort and focus to the job and provide outcomes at level with your expectations, sometimes better compared to a professional!

Transparent Communicating is the vital

While not needing to Supervise anyone and getting the work well performed in hand may seem as a blessing—handling freelancers can be hard. To make certain you get the maximum from time and effort you spend (and you don't need to do it over and over again), it's necessary that you keep a totally professional, clear relationship together, with everything out of deadlines and job requirements hauled in sharp, succinct points.

Another Fantastic tip would Be to make sure your communication is obviously recorded. A verbal pact never actually holds from the world. With freelancers, it's even more important to have something equally can consult in the event of a debate. Obtaining a contract is a very handy practice.

Don't confuse the Freelancer to get a remote employee

A distant Employee is a employee of this firm that does not necessarily have to be within the workplace, even though a freelancer/contractor, on the other hand, is somebody who operates with no employment duties—the provisions are project-based and finish with the project's end.

Remote employees are a Part of their business—they're hired in a manner they walk the conversation when they are coming in daily. But, freelancers can't be anticipated to be overly devoted to the corporation. They'll be honest towards their job and the contract provisions, but that is about it. They're not so worried about what is happening with the business, provided that the job is implemented in the desired manner and they get compensated.

Pay them

The Majority of the time, Freelancers get the work done for less cash. Nonetheless, this is somebody's alive, even if it's supplementary. Paying freelancers under the industry rate defines that you're searching for a suboptimal quality of job—and will determine just how much effort the freelancer will place into your job, if they opt to get it done.

Paying fair requires One to get a fantastic understanding of market prices, even though it largely depends upon the particulars of this job and what your budget is. You may go to several portals such as Upwork to find a feeling of the industry speed and arrive at a ballpark.

However, the best way To arrive at a good rate would be to utilize salary benchmarks to compute an hourly fee. If you aren't paying them on an hourly basis, compute the average quantity of time it might take to finish a job and determine a job speed.

Invest Time with Them

If You'd like your Freelancers to provide their very best work, you need to invest in the connection. Even if they're not just part of the group, you need to make an effort and make them feel they are.

Invite them to internet Meetings, spend some time on video calls together and encourage them in your company retreats. Should they operate from your bodily office be certain they have access to areas of your workplace such as the gym and the cafeteria so they can mingle with your own people.

These Tiny steps will Go a long way in raising their devotion to the group. In reality, freelancers often continue to function for years—more than the tenure of the typical total time employees!

If you are a freelancer

Focus on a Single Place

Freelancers can vary From those that are only dabbling into something to known specialists who few businesses can afford to employ. The trick to becoming successful as a freelancer is to create your experience in 1 area. "The more specialized you are, the more superior you are likely to control," states Rich Pearson, Upwork's Senior VP of Marketing.

For Instance, If you Are a marketing pro, don't occupy any project you may get your hands on these as content composing or societal networking marketing. Naturally, the longer spent in a special area, the greater you'll be and thus, you'll have the ability to charge higher prices.

Maintain your Career in Head

Before taking any Job, attempt to ascertain how it adds value to a career instead of how much it might cover. It is ideal to take up jobs that add value to a resume, even if they don't cover up to other endeavors. If it increases a profile, then you'll have the ability to require higher prices or a larger salary at a complete time occupation in future.

Freelance jobs are Also a means to land whole time jobs with businesses. Should they really enjoy your job, you could always approach them for a complete time job.

Locate the Right Opportunities

There are many Websites which host freelancer work opportunities. A number of the best known ones include Upwork, Freelancer and Fiverr. On the other hand, the rivalry on those platforms is ferocious and it may be hard to locate gigs that pay you well. As opposed to attempt to use to as many chances as you can, spend time using for just a couple of businesses that are the ideal match for the profile, abilities and the kinds of gigs you're searching for.

Construct your Personal Brand

The highest paid Freelancers prevent these sites like Upwork and Freelancer. Rather they invest in constructing their own private brands to obtain customers.

Write articles for best Books, develop a presence on interpersonal networking, and be certain that you have a personal site which highlights your portfolio. Investing time in developing a reputation as a specialist will permit you to find the best jobs and charge high prices.

It is also possible to begin a site . Blogging is a tried and true way of Constructing a personal brand on line. Many men and women underestimate the exponential power of blogging.

Network

Your system helps you Flourish in the independent market. A referral is most likely among the very best techniques to find the gig. In case you've got a fantastic network which may refer you, then half of your job is finished. Many businesses don't like visiting freelancer portals due to the time and effort it requires out to display the ideal candidate—a referral requires that attempt off their hands and they immediately find the appropriate fit.

Notice: Always recall 1 thing—firms cover answers, maybe hours. Therefore, as you could reverse engineer from your wages in the present job to realize how much you need to be compensated for one hour, is it important to check at the way in which the alternative adds value to this business and cost the job so. If you don't factor that in, you miss out on additional income.

Firms Utilizing the Gig Economy as Part of The Company Model

For many businesses, The Gig economy is not just about hiring freelancers. It is a part of the core business model. They're using technology and procedures to handle their own teams. Having a peek at their surgeries is rewarding since it reflects tendencies in how gigs are forming the market as a whole.

Lyft

The fastest growing Rideshare business in america, Lyft has been among the first adopters of their sharing market, wherein motorists get compensated for the amount of rides. A greater part of Lyft drivers push part time. Based on Business Insider, over 93 percent push fewer than 20 hours each week; 92 percent are employed, seeking employment, full-time students or employees; and 96 percent state flexible hours are extremely or very significant.

Lyft was the very first Firm to provide in-app tipping, together with other features like same-day obligations and cheap car rentals. What is more, it tied up with Guild to offer access to instruction to builders!

TaskRabbit

Ikea-acquired TaskRabbit is a aggregator that connects customers with those who will contribute with house maintenance services such as putting furniture together, deliveries and cleaning. How things work is rather simple—clients flag the job they should get completed, and"taskers" may pick the job nearby, deciding upon the pace at which they'll be working. Based on Forbes, TaskRabbit has just 60 full time employees but over 60,000 employees using the platform to receive jobs.

Deliveroo

UK-based Deliveroo, a Food-ordering program, ties with freelancer riders to provide restaurant orders. Individuals may register to make deliveries in their spare time. It works in over 200 cities across 13 states and has increased nearly a thousand dollars of investor funds.

Where are we headed?

In accordance with some Recent research from the McKinsey Global Instituteup to 162 million people in the USA and Europe are included in some type of independent work. This has attracted focus the way the way we operate has developed over time. But, We've Got a long way to go, also want to jointly work towards fostering a sustainable growth of the gig market,

Employers Will Need to Recognize that freelancers will develop into a main area of the work force. Thus, they can not be treated as they've been previously and need to be integrated more closely with their own teams. In the same way, freelancers will need to dedicate to their own gigs more seriously if they are to get higher prices and receive higher-quality jobs.

The gig market is Raising several questions regarding the rights of accountants and companies' obligations . Governments across many nations are considering ways to attract the gig market within the reach of regulations which will shield freelancer rights.

Firms who take proactive Actions to provide more benefits to their workers will acquire the most—as their freelancers will probably be ready to go the extra mile to provide their finest.

Conclusion

The gig market is Mainly driven by the requirement to capitalize on available resources and time, with no long-term obligations. Every business requires the very best job done, and also the best may not be accessible for a long term dedication.

Tech Has driven the development of this gig market, creating more apparently flexible opportunities for individuals to earn income, like via ride-sharing services such as Uber and Lyft, or freelancer labor fitting platforms like Taskrabbit. From those new business models have emerged exceptional business relationships that do not often match classic labor frameworks. By way of instance, employees with jobs which resemble those of ordinary workers' might be disguised as"self-employed" people,"freelancers" or"entrepreneurs" that don't have access to cxactly the very same rights and benefits lawfully because of regular workers, including freedom of association and collective bargaining. While providing ease from the delivery of services that are needed and supplying flexible financial opportunities particularly to individuals that are not able to devote to the rigidity of normal employment (for example, mothers and homemakers), the gig market has also presented serious challenges to imitating labour rights by being connected with work, enforced casualisation, cloudy hours, bad pay and involuntary overtime.

This Section investigates the negative and positive human rights consequences related to the gig market, in addition to the should re-imagine and change policy and legal rights protection frameworks so as to keep up with the times.

CHAPTER SEVEN:
USING FREELANCERS TO SAVE YOU THOUSANDS

Freelancing can be Mutually beneficial for both the contractor and the company. In an economic downturn, companies are reaping numerous advantages from builders which are providing quality work for exceptionally low rates. Presently, freelancing job is comparable to a"buyer's market" in property. Employers are outsourcing jobs to spending and freelancers 75 percent less than they would to a complete time worker. This is an unbelievable chance for new small business owners who have very little funds, but an idea that has to be introduced to market.

Search engine Optimization (search engine optimization), search engine optimization (SEM) and key word rich content will be the regions where customers are getting a substantial thing. Salaried employees doing the identical quantity of work will could be compensated five times the quantity or more for exactly the identical quantity of consultation and work. Business owners that have to construct their clientele online are actually in an edge with the services which are supplied by salespeople.

Salaried versus Freelancers

Freelancers are hired On an as required basis, whereas workers are hired and paid a salary. Freelancers supplying SEO content might be paid 25% to 75 percent less than a salaried employee, based on the standard of work supplied. Normally, companies need to change their search engine optimization content monthly or longer to keep to rank high in the significant search engines. This is a considerable investment to have somebody on staff to complete these missions yearly. A freelancer might be hired to carry out these jobs for a fraction of the price tag. Many firms using freelancers for this kind of labour save thousands.

Firms can Hire freelancers for significantly less, because almost all of these folks are desperate to get an income. Most freelancers are looking forward to a permanent position with a business or are awaiting the upcoming significant project. While they're waiting, they execute those tasks so as to keep their finances. Company owners depended on their requirement for work and extend them money to save their business money. At the time of this"green" business, company owners are cutting costs where they could.

Telecommuting

With the introduction Of cloud computing systems, customers may easily use freelancers to achieve tasks. They could collaborate on SEO articles, internet content, study or any additional work which might be outsourced. This makes it effortless to use freelancers, since they don't need to be present to get access to software or finish a project. All meetings might be held almost or through email. Businesses that use cloud computing conserve their company tens of thousands on digital assistants and personnel.

Virtual assistants can Also put together demonstrations through Microsoft PowerPoint, create graphics for sites or some other necessary correspondence. Some digital assistants even field telephone calls for companies.

How it Gains the Freelancer

Freelancers accept Tasks for less pay to maintain their skills fresh and also to cover requirements. The ones which aren't getting unemployment or have drained their retirement funds can utilize outsourcing to supplement their earnings or savings through a slow period.

Some salespeople enjoy The lifestyle since it allows them the flexibility to operate when they need, how frequently they need and where they desire. On the other hand, the lifestyle might become stressful if they aren't being paid their true worth or value. Most salespeople working for less, work long hours and numerous times a week to compensate for the smaller earnings. As time passes, freelancers might"burn " from excessive strain due to long hours and little pay. In spite of these issues, some salespeople continue the lifestyle as the other choices aren't congruent with their work styles.

The way to work with a Freelancer

Some businesses Establish good working relationships with specific freelancers and provide more extended contracts. Steady work from recognized businesses is favored by salespeople. When individuals work with reasonable men and women who know they are getting a good or service for less than they'd pay differently they like their jobs longer.

Some companies cover Less and need more than they'd of a staffed worker. This practice causes aggravation and reduces the advantages of freelancer work. The strain of working with a few businesses may cause some salespeople to turn off work. This is an advantage of being a freelancernonetheless, sometimes, that might cause the loss of considerable sums.

Freelancers must Always carry out a cost-benefit evaluation before accepting or continuing to operate with a firm on a job. If the requirements are so large that the freelancers' salary are diminished, then the job is not a viable source of revenue. Many businesses outsource jobs to other nations including India to obtain work for less cash. But, freelancers are situated domestically working to the very same salary, but have a higher cost of living. Firms must continue to keep that mind when securing freelance work for significantly less that the connection stays on amicable terms. These businesses receive the high quality work they're trying to find.

Additional Financial Advantages of Freelancers

Freelancers may be Hired for numerous jobs. Freelancers may ghost compose, edit novels, compose SEO articles, develop sites, perform research, write source code, shoot photos, consult, work in earnings or other jobs which are required temporarily. These folks are hired as contractors. Therefore, companies don't need to pay unemployment, supplement , provide other advantages or manage paperwork connected with a complete time worker. Firms save considerable sums of money and effort by employing a builder instead of a full-time worker.

Start-up Businesses Find contractors appealing since they save on those costs. New legislation are making it cheaper to hire workers, but contractors or freelancers are still cheaper despite the close $9,000 incentive given by the authorities for hiring certain kinds of workers.

How to Get Freelance Jobs

There are many reasons Why people decide to freelance. Some reasons are your own boss, to operate at home or to make additional cash. However, how can you get freelance jobs and is that a fantastic time ?

What's the freelancer Marketplace?

Before deciding to become A freelancer (also referred to as a service supplier), it is very good to understand the health of the freelance industry. What's it a fantastic time to freelancer? This could look a little counterintuitive, but through periods such as we are currently undergoing, freelance jobs really grow. So the easy answer to this question is,'yes'. Freelance jobs are on the market, you will find more than you believe, they simply have to get found.

Is freelancing for me personally?

To paraphrase a Well-known term, if freelancing is well worth doing, it is worth doing well. And if you are not geared up for a freelancer then there is no point in getting one!

To Assist You understand Whether outsourcing is for you, ask yourself these questions:

- Can you like working for different companies or other men and women?
- Are you currently a self-starter, able to oversee your work and your own time?
- Can you pay attention ?
- Can you finish what you start and enjoy everything you do?
- These queries are The exact very same ones an employer might want to discover answers to before supplying a permanent job to a possible worker and it is not any different for freelance jobs.

So if you are searching To become a successful freelancer, then your own replies to each one the aforementioned should be,"yes". Freelancing could be a way to make additional cash, but if you would like to make a success out of it and also keep your earnings, then it is ideal to leave a track list full of happy occupation suppliers.

Which abilities or Service do I want to freelancer?

There is not a particular Ability or set of abilities necessary to acquire freelance jobs. And need for freelance services fluctuates. There are helpful websites which provide need info, for example itjobswatch and jobstats, however you might also obtain helpful information by simply searching and counting the amount of freelance jobs reported by your favorite search engine.

But do not be Discouraged if your ability or support is not popular with Google or Bing. In reality, obtaining a skill or agency which has low need puts you at a prime place on the current market, especially if not many different freelancers have your ability or can provide your services.

And for certain, if a Company or person can micro outsource that, then it could be freelanced! So just bear this in mind.

However, as a direct, freelancer Tasks include data entry, CCTV monitoring, online advertising, parcel couriering, event preparation, telephone calling, customer support, gardening, event preparation, post writing and Site development. So abilities are often as varied as scanning or data entry and video observation to composing and internet development.

Where to Search for freelancing jobs?

Job boards are still an Obvious place to begin. But, job boards do not specialise in micro outsourced tasks, which would be the sort of jobs you are seeking to get as a freelancer. Additionally, job boards catch CVs rather than solutions, which might not really help you in the event you've got a normal CV that will show you have done more than 1 thing of your lifetime.

There are expert Websites which could allow you to get freelance jobs. With these websites, you will have the ability to publicize your support, not your own CV, and you are going to have the ability to emphasize your relevant skills and expertise. You will also have the ability to socialize with project providers, which will let you discuss project requirements and your abilities, and work together once you have the job!

Finding Freelance Work

To all those of you that Believe that outsourcing is simple: you might wish to believe again. There haven't been more salespeople from the market, and they're frequently stiff competition. Nevertheless, the fantastic thing is that there haven't been more companies searching for freelancers, and there are lots of means to reach them. For exactly the identical reason there are several freelancers available on the marketplace, there are businesses taking advantage of the manpower. Employees tend to be laid off because the business can not afford to get that specific skill set on employees full-time. But they still have jobs that need those skills. By using salespeople to finish projects rather than full-time employees, companies can cut prices. Freelancers simply must understand how to approach such businesses.

A Lot of People start out Freelancing believing that perform will somehow only land in their hands. However, it takes some time to develop contacts and get your name on the market. Freelancers ought to have a small nest egg saved to turn to in case you have problems finding work at first. Needless to say, when beginning sourcing it's crucial to recognize your most important skills. By specifying exactly what you you allow companies understand what needs they could meet you. You can make a list of the top 3 things you do , and be certain that they are simple to see on your resume, your own site, and your site if you have one.

Even If You're new to Freelancing and it may appear intimidating, do not despair. There are plenty of sources of information and tips on the world wide web that will assist you find your way. The freelancer community is usually very receptive to sharing their own experiences with individuals that are new to the freelance industry. They have loads of information to contribute to brand new franchisees. There are a large number of sites which are packed to the brim with helpful information for salespeople.

You Might Even be Wondering whether there's an independent requirement for your individual skill. While previously freelancing was largely relegated to photography and writing, there's now part time consulting and contract work for virtually every business. This is particularly true in the present financial climate, where companies can't afford to own as many full-time employees. Firms are in need of several skill sets, and the secret is to locate what firms are needing your skills. 1 way this may be achieved is by checking out business sites to find out what has to be performed, then contact them and let them know you have the abilities necessary for the job.

With all the Technological progress of the previous 20 decades, finding freelance work has gotten infinitely simpler. There are hundreds and hundreds of websites which show freelancer job openings and permit you to place your data online for companies to test out. A number of the more popular websites include ODesk.com, Elance.com and Guru.com. It's currently an immensely simpler procedure to join with companies and begin freelancer work. They save time and permit companies to target applicable freelance employees .

As Stated above, But there have also been more people searching for freelance job so that it is worth it to make yourself stand out. A specialist site is vital (obviously much more so for web designers). It demonstrates to prospective employers that you're a freelancer that they ought to take seriously. It is often the first place business look to find out more about you. Freelancers should contain descriptions of certain abilities, past work experience, and when possible, examples of your work together with testimonials. A site might also be helpful, a means to demonstrate your experience in your area. You could even seek and provide freelancing information on your website.

Top Reasons Why Folks Freelance

Freelancing is now The career option for an increasing number of men and women in the united kingdom and around Europe. This report explains the best 7 reasons why folks think about sourcing a career prospect.

What's a freelancer?

A freelancer, too Called a contractor or service provider, is somebody who provides their services for an agreed period in exchange for a fee. Freelancers are independent of those companies or individuals who hire their own services. Normally, freelancers operate on short-term contracts, and but contracts can vary in duration and may be and are usually extended

Why do folks freelance?

We have assembled 7 Of the best reasons why folks freelancer:

1. To be your personal boss. Freelancing is one of most effective approaches to begin your own company and companies are often as varied as you can imagine. Personally, I provided IT services but freelancers Provide a diverse set of solutions, some of which contain:

- event management
- Tracking and proof-reading
- online-marketing and SEO
- book-keeping and bookkeeping

Being your own boss Also permits you to choose the number of hours you work, when in the year and from which places.

2. As a lifestyle choice. Many people today like new challenges and might find working for the exact same company over several years past. Freelancing permits you to work for various businesses and people, experience new project challenges and create career opportunities.

3. To journey. If you like Travelling, then freelancing can permit you to do precisely that and get paid! Freelance opportunities can happen locally, regionally or globally. If you are eager to travel then you will have more opportunities open to you. Within my career, I worked throughout the United Kingdom in Milton Keynes, Cardiff, Hemel Hempstead and assorted places in Central London. Back in Europe, I worked in Austria and Germany, and globally, I worked in Australia and Brazil.

4. To operate remotely or From house. If your preference is to work remotely or from home afterward freelancing provides this flexibility and salespeople may enjoy a prosperous business doing exactly that. The vital thing to ask is the work you want to do be performed remotely or from your property. If the solution is yes then there will be companies and people seeking to employ your abilities. Website development is a favorite action but many others include data entry, virtual help, post writing, translation, online & personal lodging, etc.

5. As a Fast way back into work. If you are between jobs then getting into permanent employment may take a few months. Freelancers could be hired and get their first payment in a couple weeks of first contact by an employer or broker. What's more, some contracts may result in permanent employment because the hiring company seeks to keep your services.

6. As a Fast way to Earn cash. Freelancers may be compensated not just faster and frequently than permanent employees but also a superior for not being in a company's citizenship or to get working on a short term job. This permits a freelancer to make a great deal more in a specified period compared to a permanent employee doing similar work, which might be employed to rapidly repay a credit card or to get a long overdue vacation.

7. To gain expertise and specialise. Employed as a freelancer permits you to grow and use your professional skills more completely, which working to the exact same firm may not provide. Thus, by focusing on various contracts for various companies, freelancers can easily gain expertise and become subject matter experts in their chosen area.

These are Only a few Of the reasons why folks become freelancers. You could have a different motive from those discussed. If you believe freelancing is best for you then why don't you give it a try. I did!

Ways to begin?

Upload your CV into a Appropriate website. A number of the more recognizable sites comprise reed, Cardiff Jobs, Workthing, Gumtree, StepStone and ClickAJob. These sites, however, concentrate on collecting CVs, which might not perform your ceremony justice. Furthermore, they don't concentrate on micro outsourced tasks, the kind of jobs you are seeking to do.

Fortunately, are Sites that specialise in marketing your services. On these websites, you will have the ability to promote your services, specifying your abilities, work place (should you prefer working from home), hourly or daily rate and so forth. And unlike with job boards, you will have the ability to make contact job suppliers to, e.g., describe job requirements and affirm tasks, as soon as you've got the job!

How to Pick the Ideal Freelancer

Whether you are a Company or company looking for a graphic designer or digital assistant, there is no lack of highly qualified salespeople that are available to complete any kind of job possible. Irrespective of your market market or business, outsourcing your job to freelancers is a excellent way that will assist you build, grow and maintain your company.

But when Selecting a Freelancer, there are a number of things that you ought to know to ensure you pick the ideal freelancer potential and your job is finished to your satisfaction.

Finding A Freelancer

There a hundreds of Freelance job marketplaces where you are able to find highly skilled freelancers in every market imaginable from post writing to digital assistants. These marketplaces permit you to register as a company and place your job for a little charge.

When creating your Freelance job, you'll get an chance to create a job name and description. The job name should be a brief review of the undertaking. The job description must describe your project in detail, lists specific conditions which you have and express any expectations. For example, in the event that you just need certain accountants, then you are able to list that on your job description.

Although there are Normally places where you are able to list your budget and time for completion, you are able to reiterate or describe these items in the job description too.

As Soon as You've finished The particulars of your job such as the funding, time to finish and description, you will be prepared to post your job for seeing by freelancers.

When posting your Project, be certain that you pick a class that correctly identifies your kind of job. If your job is linked to article writing, it needs to be submitted in that class or a comparable person. This is vital since most freelancer job marketplaces make it possible for freelancers to get emails each time a job is submitted to a class to which they're subscribed. Properly categorizing your job insures the ideal freelancers will bid on your job.

Selecting The Right Freelancer

Once your job has Been submitted for bidding and salespeople have put bids in your job, you need to identify a few candidates based upon your own criteria.

If appropriate such as In the instance of an essay writing endeavor, you need to ask to view samples. For graphic or web design jobs, you might want to ask to assess the freelancer's portfolio.

Most freelance job Marketplaces make it possible for freelancers to be rated or reviewed on past jobs. Ratings and reviews are important steps of a freelancer's reliability and ability in completing previous jobs and shouldn't be overlooked when determining a freelancer with whom to perform. Ratings and reviews are typically a fantastic indicator of the sort of service you will receive.

Before selecting a Provider, you need to communicate with the freelancer so as to clarify your job requirements. Communication with the freelancer before the job also can help ascertain whether the freelancer will be receptive to your own emails. If a freelancer is not receptive to your communication before being granted a job, you should not anticipate the freelancer will be responsive after being given the job.

Understanding How to select A freelancer can allow you to avoid a few of the pitfalls which might happen from picking out the incorrect freelancer. Pick the best freelancer and you're going to have somebody that will assist you build, grow and maintain your company.

Freelancers' Futures are Intelligent

The new year brings Very good reasons to be happy and smile as it forecasts that salespeople could have a bright and prosperous future ahead. Recently a survey was conducted through an online services market for professionals searching for freelance jobs. The poll demonstrated that outsourcing business could radically increase in the coming years from over 800 freelance professionals since a whopping 79 percent of respondents anticipate their freelancer business to raise in 2010. Surprisingly from these surveyed 59 percent of freelancers favor Freelancing to Full-Time Employment. This clearly says the outsourcing sector will see a significant boom in the coming years which means there are far more amount of freelance jobs will be accessible to franchisees throughout the world.

Professionals from Around the globe in virtually every business sector are searching for freelance-projects since they can not rely on their whole time jobs . The insecurity of losing a project could be one of the motives of developing demand of salespeople.

The international economic Recession could be one reason supporting the rising need of salespeople throughout the world. 18 percent of professionals that participated in the poll thought that the current loss of a project because their principal reason for freelancing, and another 36% utilizing outsourcing as a means to supplement earnings from a fulltime occupation. Just 29 percent of respondents believed freelancing to function as the principal job or company. The liberty can also be one of the rationale salespeople choose outsourcing because they operate from home and set their time alongside the capability to control their own fate when raising their earnings potential.

Still another reason as many Professionals think that outsourcing would grow as numerous small and massive organizations are also looking ahead to outsource their significant freelancer jobs missions to freelancers. They would like to outsource their heart and non-core duties to freelancers as 57 percent of the survey respondents believe that the primary rationale is to"cut prices or reduce employees".

This obviously explains That freelancers have more freelance jobs forthcoming their manners within the upcoming few decades. We expect that freelancers locate jobs and develop their business in the not too distant future. Please discuss with us what are the predictions for outsourcing livelihood; also share your opinions and suggestions on precisely the exact same.

Being a freelancer only indicate that you work on your own and offer a service or gift that may be outsourced. There are quite a few solutions that could be outsourced, these services include writing, programming, web design, search engine optimisation, etc.. Services like these generally can be done from a remote place without the necessity of a neighborhood onsite presence. This being the situation makes outsourcing very attractive as a supplier and as a purchaser.

It is almost obvious How suppliers gain from freelancing and chances of freelance jobs. With no need to arrive on site this imply freelancer suppliers can operate at home or distant and save travel expenditures. Additionally, it entails that the freelancer provider isn't limited to just local opportunities. With the capacity to make it to the world through the Web it might seem being a freelancer supplier is a smart career move. If an independent supplier can generate a name for themselves then the chances may get infinite. Creating a title into your target market requires commitment and time. You need to continue to cultivate your talent and abilities since this can set the stage to your freelancing career route. When freelancing there are several methods to find freelance jobs. Among the most effective methods of locating and procuring freelance opportunities is by simply being a member of freelancer job boards, for example RemoteGurus.com, GetAFreelancer.com, and Elance.com.

These freelance job Boards are generally frequented by people seeking outsourced talent, however the Catch 22 is that these job boards can also be frequented by rivals who are Also competing for the exact same freelance jobs.

These freelance job boards function At a reverse auction fashion, buyers post projects and jobs while freelance Suppliers bid on the tasks and jobs in hopes to be chosen as the winning bidder. Since its competitive platform for a freelancer You Have to be Competitive with your own rates. Employing these job boards you will Probably need To shortchange yourself as a way to win awards, but the trade-off is that will Most likely continue to locate and get new job.

The freelance job Boards are fantastic for building your new and visibility for a freelance. Since you continue to construct a name for yourself and your recognition on the planks grow your standing will start to precede itself. The freelance job boards have been equipped using a rating system that allow buyers that you work for to speed your ability and solutions, the more evaluations and also the higher the score the more likely you'll land new jobs consistently. Possessing large number of favorable evaluations also indicate that you will likely be in a position to bid higher (without shortchanging yourself) about the jobs that have a fantastic prospect of winning the job. The key will be to maintain a respectable name and your company will keep growing in time.

Buyers benefit at a Number of methods by outsourcing their tasks and jobs to gifted professionals. For a small business owner or home employee, outsourcing to distant freelancers is an perfect solution. Outsourcing to remote and telecommuting professionals imply that you don't have to get an onsite physical speech or lease additional office area, you save on overhead costs. Utilizing reverse auction-styled project boards for example RemoteGurus.com, GetAFreelancer.com, and Elance.com you'll have the ability to appraise your freelancer provider before taking them as the winning bidder. You'll have access to look at their evaluation history and consumer profile, you ought to use this information to your benefit—it is called doing your homework.

These Kind of job Boards allow you to locate freelance providers in a controlled environment and helps reduce the probability of being ripped off. These sort of job boards enable the purchaser to put money into escrow before releasing the funds to the freelancer provider. Escrow simply make it possible for one and the freelancer provider to have a just and positive encounter without being taken for a ride. The purchaser can't cancel payment after in escrow, they could simply send (accept) the payment to be published into the freelancer supplier. The supplier has the choice to cancel payment after in escrow (cheque payment will yield the money to the purchaser—leaving the supplier unpaid), however the freelancer provider can't send (accept) the payment.

By both parties Sharing this duty it puts hands into every party hand. In the event the job isn't finished to your satisfaction afterward as the purchaser you merely don't release the funds into the supplier from escrow. This also protects you from getting screwed out of cash. In the majority of cases if the supplier didn't finish the job to gratification they'll cancel the payment and funds return to you (the purchaser). If for any reason there's a dispute then you're able to involve the job board owner to take care of the dispute and reunite your funds for the accounts. It is a truly win-win circumstance.

CONCLUSION

In Summary, as a Freelancer supplier you'll be well on your way to being a desired freelancer should you employ the freelance job boards because your springboard for developing your name and manufacturer. My advice would be to run low and sell yourself short at first simply to get tasks, jobs, and expertise. As soon as you've assembled your name and score then you can begin raising your bids and inquiring for the going rate. Work for testimonials in the start and you'll be on your way to working for cash. In terms of buyers, provided that you do your homework and check supplier reviews then make use of escrow for obligations, you will raise buyer protection on your own. Employing freelance job boards you may find professional, quality, and very affordable freelance providers that are capable and dependable. Best of luck to you.

Don't miss out!

Visit the website below and you can sign up to receive emails whenever Daniel D. Coffman publishes a new book. There's no charge and no obligation.

https://books2read.com/r/B-A-VRLAB-OIEOC

Did you love *Gig Economy: Opportunities to Work Online with Freelance or Remote Smart Working*? Then you should read *Freelance Consulting: Provide Services to High Ticket Customers. Build and Grow Your own Gig Empire.*[1] by Daniel D. Coffman!

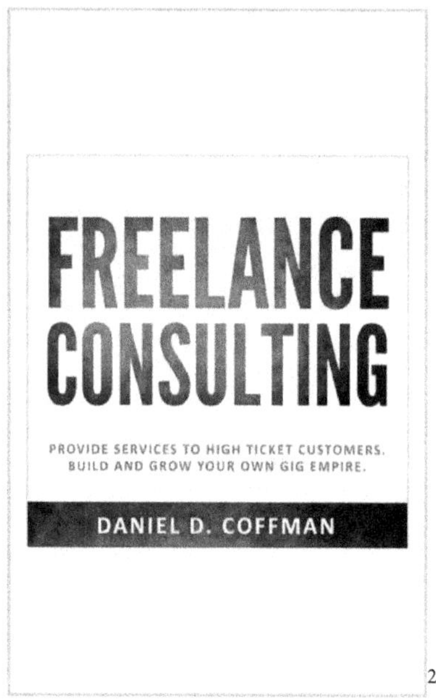

[2]

How to take the headache out of starting your own Freelance Consulting Business.

Are you tired of working for others?Have you always been dreaming of starting your own business and being your own boss?Do your friends always turn to you for advice?

If your answer to all these questions is yes, then, starting your own consulting business is something you definitely should do.

Nowadays, running a successful business has never been more complex and the need for good consultants has never been greater.

A consultant's only job is to provide good advice. Nothing more, nothing less. And, in this day and age, almost anyone can be a consultant. All you need

---

1. https://books2read.com/u/mgRyB6

2. https://books2read.com/u/mgRyB6

is to be good at helping others and find the industry you're interested in. There isn't some secret gift that will make one consultant more successful than the other. However, there is one skill that separates a good consultant from a bad consultant.

What separates a good consultant from a bad consultant is a passion and drive for excellence. Oh, and one more thing! Every good consultant must be knowledgeable about the subject they are consulting in.

Here is what you can learn from this book:

The easiest way get your freelance consulting business up and running 11 strategies for making customers come to you *9 surefire tactics that will help you boost your business* Top tools every freelance business must have *The greatest mistakes consulting business owners must avoid at all cost...* and much more!

Starting any business is a challenge, but starting a business where your goal is to help others run their own is doubly challenging. **This book will help you prepare yourself for running a business on your own and it will guide you every step of the way!**

The time has finally come for you to become independent and start your own business. The tips and tricks you find in this book will undoubtedly guide you to success!

Also by Daniel D. Coffman

Freelance Consulting: Provide Services to High Ticket Customers. Build and Grow Your own Gig Empire.

Gig Economy: Opportunities to Work Online with Freelance or Remote Smart Working

Work Online: Become a Solopreneur, Start Working Remotely. The Complete Guide to Grow Your Company on the Internet.

About the Author

Daniel D. Coffman has over 20 years of experience as a consultant with various large consulting firms and as an independent. His professional expertise spans more than 50 different industries in which he has worked as a consultant for his clients. He has seen everything from the smallest one-man operation to the largest corporation.

About the Publisher

CREATIVITY ¦ FUN ¦ EXPERTISE

Our imprint Creafe Publishing, where creativity meets expertise, is your destination for a captivating array of books. Our extensive collection features a harmonious blend of non-fiction treasures and engaging fiction gems. We believe that learning should be an enjoyable adventure, and our commitment to 'Creativity ¦ Fun ¦ Expertise' is evident in every page we produce. Explore our catalog to discover knowledge and entertainment like never before. With Creafe Publishing, your reading journey is bound to be a delightful and enlightening experience.